Praise for Technology for Classroom and Online Learning

"I think this is a good book with thorough contents regarding all aspects of the IT (Information Technology) we are facing these days. I do recommend this book to those educators who are not familiar with computers and its related peripheral devices. It would give a complete understanding of how these devices work and how they are interfaced with one another." —**Rex Wong**, PhD, assistant professor in Electrical Engineering sector, Engineering and Technology Department, Vaughn College of Aeronautics and Technology

"We live in an engineered world, and technology is a part of everything we do. Yet less than 5% of the nearly 2 million bachelors' degrees awarded annually in the United States are in engineering fields. This new book provides an important resource for achieving broader technical literacy in our society." —**A. Galip Ulsoy**, C.D. Mote, Jr. Distinguished University Professor and the William Clay Ford Professor of Manufacturing, University of Michigan, Ann Arbor, Michigan

"The authors have written a succinct and comprehensive approach to navigating the ever-changing educational technology world. The role of the technology teacher is critical to the future of educational technology and this book is a practical and understandable resource. I highly recommend this book." —**Christopher Lilly**, PhD, chair, department of educational technology, Concordia University Chicago

"The authors provide an excellent basis for understanding technology. I'm confident that this book will provide a positive contribution to education." —**Ken Reddy**, president, Reddysoft, Inc.

"The authors have truly captured the essence of technology education that is well written and insightful. The book is written in such a way as to make using technology simple, giving helpful hints and step-by-step guides. I highly recommend this book as a must read for leaders." —**Richard G. Richter**, EdD, ABD, director of instructional design, assistant professor instructional technology, Concordia University Chicago

"This book will greatly assist the professor possessing rich experience within their teaching passion, who may be nontechnical. The elements within will be a bridge for the professor to get and stay current with core and latest technology tools. I highly recommend this book for such educators." —**Peter McGeehan**, services operations manager, American Digital Corporation

"This book provides a very practical, thorough overview of technology integration in the classroom. I see this book being very valuable for teachers looking to use technology." —**Andrew Tawfik**, PhD, assistant professor, educational technology, research and assessment, Northern Illinois University

"This book is ideal for all educators. It provides a perfect balance of technical details with a high-level explanation of computer technology in an easy-to-comprehend manner, without the need for a technical background." —**Arthur B. Williams**, author, *The Analog Filter and Circuit Design Handbook*

"The authors have written a highly accessible and comprehensive resource for educators who wish to continue to learn and improve their use of technology to enhance instruction. This book delivers invaluable understanding and guidance." —**Donna A. Blaess**, PhD, associate professor, leadership and professional studies, Concordia University Chicago

"Using technology as an educator is no longer an option, it is an imperative! This book is a practical and understandable resource. I highly recommend this book to all educators who want to excel in using technology. Outstanding!" —**Donald F. Gately**, EdD, principal, Jericho Middle School, Jericho, New York

"The authors of this book have produced a very practical and easily understandable resource for administrators, teachers, and curriculum developers who are committed to the application of technology for the improvement of instruction and learning outcomes. I recommend this book to all dedicated educational practitioners." —**Harry L. Bowman**, president emeritus, Council on Occupational Education; Trustee and journal editorial board member, ATEA

"This volume will be an indispensable guidebook for teachers engaging with technology to bring learning opportunities into today's technologically rich classrooms." —**Kevin J. Brandon**, EdD, dean, College of Education, Concordia University Chicago

"In a world of rapidly changing technology, as well as a rapidly changing approaches to using technology, good resources that explain the 'how-to' and 'what-for' are hard to find. This book provides a thorough introduction to specific tools, techniques, and problem-solving strategies. It is a great resource for students and educators, alike." —**Ami N. Erickson**, PhD, dean of Ag, Culinary, Engineering, Math and Science, Northern Wyoming Community College

"This book offers excellent and practical guidance for the technophobe, yet explains concepts that seasoned tech-heads should know (but are afraid to ask)." —**Christian V. Hauser**, PhD, assistant professor of music, Concordia University Chicago

"As a long time adult educator and faculty member in the area of human development, this text is outstanding in terms of practicality and understandability, especially for those who work in the 'softer skill' areas." —**Jane A. Hildenbrand**, MS, program chair and professor, Ivy Tech Community College

"This book is a well-organized and comprehensive approach to the understanding of the modern computer technologies and its peripherals. The authors have covered the philosophical and its application aspect of the computer-base technologies as a tool in various areas of its analytical, visual, construction and communication tools. Highly recommended as a source for educators." —**Hovhannes John Mardirossian**, physicist and retired member of technical staff at Bell Laboratories, president and chairman, Technology and Education, Armenian Engineers and Scientist of America NY–NJ Section

"This is an excellent book. The authors have truly captured the essence of technology education that is well written and insightful. I recommend this book to all educators who want to excel in using technology." —**Mike Kendiroglu**, MS, professional engineer, retired Philips Electronics N.A., Senior Design Engineer

"The role of the technology teacher is critical to the future of educational technology and this book is a practical and understandable resource. I highly recommend this book." —**Craig A. Schilling**, EdD, advisor, Digital Schools LP, Salinas, CA

"This text enables each teacher and student to integrate technology with teaching and learning." —**Ron Warwick**, EdD, educational leadership, Concordia University

"This important book brings needed illumination and practical application to the growing relationship of Technology for Non-Technology Educators." —**Robert N. L. Browning**, founder and CEO, Success Solutions International, Oceanside, California

"If you have questions about effective pedagogical approaches to using technology, this book is a practical and understandable resource. The authors provide an excellent basis for understanding technology. I highly recommend this book." —**Robert K. Wilhite**, EdD, professor and chair, department of leadership, Concordia University Chicago

"In today's knowledge-based era it has become a challenge for educators to keep abreast with advances in technology. The professional and technical currency of educators plays an important role in promoting teaching and learning. In this book the authors have provided a primer for understanding technology for nontechnical educators by explaining in simple language the complex technological concepts. I hope this book will help educators to enhance their understanding of technology for enriching the teaching and learning processes." —**Ahmed S. Khan**, PhD, senior professor, College of Engineering & Information Sciences, DeVry University, Addison, IL

"The authors' book is a must-read for educators who want to excel at using technology in their classes." —**Claudia Santin**, PhD, dean, and professor of leadership, College of Business, Concordia University Chicago

Technology for Classroom and Online Learning

THE CONCORDIA UNIVERSITY CHICAGO LEADERSHIP SERIES
An Educational Series from Rowman & Littlefield

Series Editor: Daniel R. Tomal

Education leaders have many titles and positions in American schools today: professors, K–12 teachers, district and building administrators, teacher coaches, teacher evaluators, directors, coordinators, staff specialists, etc. More than ever, educators need practical and proven educational and leadership resources to stay current and advance the learning of students.

Concordia University Chicago Leadership Series is a unique resource that addresses this need. The authors of this series are award-winning authors and scholars who are both passionate theorists and practitioners of this valuable collection of works. They give realistic and real-life examples and strategies to help all educators inspire and make a difference in school improvement and student learning that get results.

This Leadership Series consists of a variety of distinctive books on subjects of school change, research, completing advanced degrees, school administration, leadership and motivation, business finance and resources, human resource management, challenging students to learn, action research for practitioners, the teacher as a coach, school law and policies, ethics, and many other topics that are critical to modern educators in meeting the emerging and diverse students of today. These books also align with current federal, state, and various association accreditation standards and elements.

Staying current and building the future require the knowledge and strategies presented in these books. The Leadership Series originator, Daniel R. Tomal, PhD, is an award-winning author who has published over 18 books and 200 articles and studies, and is a highly sought-after speaker and educational researcher. He along with his coauthors provide a wealth of educational experience, proven strategies that can help all educators aspire to be the best they can be in meeting the demands of modern educational leadership.

Titles in the Series
Challenging Students to Learn: How to Use Effective Leadership and Motivation Tactics
Action Research for Educators
Discipline by Negotiation: Methods for Managing Student Behavior
Action Research for Educators, Second Edition
Managing Human Resources and Collective Bargaining
Resource Management for School Administrators: Optimizing Fiscal, Facility, and Human Resources
Leading School Change: Maximizing Resources for School Improvement
How to Finish and Defend Your Dissertation: Strategies to Complete the Professional Practice Doctorate
The Teacher Leader: Core Competencies and Strategies for Effective Leadership
The Challenge for School Leaders: A New Way of Thinking about Leadership
Supervision and Evaluation for Learning and Growth: Strategies for Teacher and School Leader Improvement
Grant Writing: Practical Strategies for Scholars and Professionals
Technology for Classroom and Online Learning: An Educator's Guide to Bits, Bytes, and Teaching

Technology for Classroom and Online Learning

An Educator's Guide to Bits, Bytes, and Teaching

Samuel M. Kwon, Daniel R. Tomal,
and Aram S. Agajanian

ROWMAN & LITTLEFIELD
Lanham • Boulder • New York • London

Published by Rowman & Littlefield
A wholly owned subsidiary of The Rowman & Littlefield Publishing Group, Inc.
4501 Forbes Boulevard, Suite 200, Lanham, Maryland 20706
www.rowman.com

Unit A, Whitacre Mews, 26-34 Stannary Street, London SE11 4AB

British Library Cataloguing in Publication Information Available

Library of Congress Cataloging-in-Publication Data Available

ISBN 978-1-4758-1543-6 (cloth : alk. paper)
ISBN 978-1-4758-1544-3 (paper : alk. paper)
ISBN 978-1-4758-1545-0 (electronic)

∞™ The paper used in this publication meets the minimum requirements of American National Standard for Information Sciences—Permanence of Paper for Printed Library Materials, ANSI/NISO Z39.48-1992.

Printed in the United States of America

Contents

Foreword

Ensuring teachers are well prepared for the classroom they will soon be leading is a top priority for these authors. They listened to their students and learned that there were gaps that needed to be filled prior to sending the students out to obtain teaching positions. The result is the wonderfully organized text that presents the more technical aspects of managing a digital classroom steeped in the International Society of Technology in Education standards (ISTE).

Each chapter aligns with ISTE standards and reinforces the depth of knowledge teachers must acquire prior to their first job.

Dr. Kecia Ray
International Society for Technology in Education, Board Chair 2013–2015
Executive Director,
Center for Digital Education

Acknowledgments

Many people merit recognition. To begin, my coauthors of this book deserve many thanks. Dan Tomal led this effort by first inviting me to participate in the writing of this book in the summer of 2014. While we were all very busy with preparations for the new academic year, his enthusiasm and clear vision for a book that could truly help teachers was very persuasive. His leadership and hard work were critical elements in this project.

Aram Agajanian was a warm and friendly coauthor, who happened to also be highly skilled and knowledgeable. His technical know-how and experience are evident in his writing and many contributions to this text.

Special acknowledgement should be offered to other groups of people who enabled the writing of this book by both helping me learn and grow, and by creating an environment that supported and encouraged creative work. Ardelle Pate, Louvenia Hollins, Richard Richter, Scott Schuth, Michael Sukowski, Andrew Tawfik, Jeffrey Hunt, Christopher Lilly, Carolyn Theard-Griggs, and Carol Reiseck were part of an educational technology department at Concordia University Chicago that truly cared about helping teachers learn and become better educators.

I learned a lot from each of them as we worked together to create and share resources and ideas for our students and for the field. Thomas Jandris, the dean of our college, and Margaret Trybus, associate dean, set the tone for our local academic community creating an environment that emphasized innovation and quality work.

I would also like to thank Louis Gomez at UCLA, who was my dissertation committee chair and mentor at Northwestern University. The guidance he provided, and the research, development, and support opportunities he enabled me to be a part of, were essential to my professional growth. His innovative thinking on using teaching and learning with technology to serve urban youth allowed me to work in schools in very special situations with teachers and administrators. I can't imagine how that would have been possible without his leadership.

My colleagues and other mentors at the time, including Kimberley Gomez, Ken Rose, Vera Kemeny, Peter Wardrip, Martin Block, Claudia Hindo, and Margaret Pligge, also helped me learn and grow as an educator. I appreciated the opportunity to work with them.

Finally, I need to thank family members for their support in this endeavor. My wife, Susan, and two daughters, Abigail and Jane, were always ready to provide hugs of encouragement. The two sets of grandparents helped entertain my daughters on days when I needed a little extra work time, and aunts and uncles Sarah, Elizabeth, Tae, and Young were also ready to encourage and support as needed. Thank you everyone!

Samuel M. Kwon, PhD

The authors wish to thank the many organizations and people who contributed to the development of this book. We express our appreciation to the companies that provided information and illustrations such as Dell Inc., Apple Inc., Microsoft Corporation, and the International Society for Technology in Education (ISTE). And, most importantly, a special thanks to Ken Reddy, Reddysoft, Inc., for his review.

We wish to thank Rowman & Littlefield Education for being the publishing partner of this work. Aram Agajanian would like to acknowledge the infinite advice, knowledge, and support of Dr. Ahmed Khan. He also appreciates his wife Serpouhi's love and continuous encouragement.

INTRODUCTION

The use of educational technology in K–12 schools and higher education degree programs continues to grow across the country. Most K–12 and university educators use some form of technology to enhance their teaching. Yet many educators at all levels of education continue to struggle to understand, maintain, troubleshoot, and use technology to its fullest capacity. This is due in part to a lack of understanding of some foundational technical and pedagogical concepts.

Many K–12 teachers are given computers equipped with various hardware and software, only to find it difficult to fully understand how to use these new tools. Beyond regular operation of the devices, effectively integrating technology into daily learning activities and the broader curriculum is even more challenging. Technical support and professional development are often needed to help educators better use the new resources that are now available to them.

This book is designed for all educators, including those in K–12 schools and university settings, and those serving as professional development coaches. This book will help educators improve their understanding of core technology concepts that enable the proficient use and troubleshooting of hardware, software, and computer networks. It will help educators improve their understanding of foundational pedagogical concepts and best practices for designing and implementing technology-enhanced lessons in traditional classroom and online situations.

Specific questions often asked by educators are addressed. These include questions like how do computers and networks work? What are electrical and power requirements of electronic devices? How can educators do simple and common troubleshooting of technology devices? What are the key issues related to computer security for schools? What are cloud technologies? What are the best approaches to using technology for supporting teaching and learning?

Chapter 1 begins by addressing the history of computer and electronic technologies. The chapter covers several topics related to hardware essentials and software essentials. Several examples of current technologies are included in these chapters. The chapter ends with a case study exercise. Additional discussion questions are provided with a list of relevant references.

The next chapter presents the fundamentals of electricity and electronics. Having a good understanding of how technology works can be beneficial to an educator. Topics in this chapter include understanding electronic components, electronic technology applications, and understanding methods of troubleshooting. The design of a computer circuit is presented and explained so that readers can understand its basic operation. Several practical examples are also given in this chapter to assist in the maintaining, operating, and troubleshooting of electronics.

The third chapter deals with computer peripherals. This chapter provides an overview of peripherals, interface technologies, software drivers, and the basic troubleshooting of peripheral devices. The important features of popular peripherals like printers, hard drives, and monitors are discussed, and approaches to addressing common problems with these devices are also explained.

The fourth chapter covers computer networking. An overview of networking in general is provided as well as an introduction to networking devices and software. Cloud technology is explained and basic network security issues are discussed. Finally, creating usable networks in schools is explained and strategies for troubleshooting and maintaining those networks are provided.

Chapter 5 covers the topic of computing platforms. The important characteristics that define a computing platform are explained. The strengths and weaknesses of several popular platforms are compared, and the appropriateness of each of the platforms for use in school situations is discussed. A case study along with exercises and discussion questions are provided to give the reader practice in applying the content of this chapter.

The next chapter covers the topic of security and maintenance. Several areas are covered, such as an overview of security and maintenance, physical security threats and countermeasures, and software threats and countermeasures. Also included in this chapter are recommendations for physical and software maintenance. The end of the chapter includes a summary, case study, and several exercises.

The seventh chapter focuses on the use of technology in teaching and learning activities. An overview of the main philosophical perspectives on the use of technology for teaching and learning is provided. Specific categories of computer technologies for supporting construction, analysis, visualization, communication, and collaboration are described, and the value they add to learning activities is discussed. Several models and strategies for integrating technology into teaching and learning activities are explained. The chapter concludes with a case study where readers can apply their understanding of educational technology to a case situation.

Chapter 8 addresses online and blended learning. Topics covered in this chapter include the benefits and trade-offs of online learning environments, the potential strengths of blended learning situations, approaches to designing online and blended units, and best practices for teaching in online settings. Theoretical models for analyzing the effectiveness of online designs, as well as strategies for supporting online communities, are explained.

FEATURES OF THE BOOK

This book is succinctly written and an easy read for undergraduate students, graduate students, practicing teachers, technology coaches, and school administrators. This book is unique in that it provides many engaging examples that can help educators understand basic technology devices, troubleshooting, operations, and technology-enhanced instruction. Each chapter's objectives are aligned with the International Society for Technology in Education (ISTE) professional organizational standards. The ISTE standards for technology coaches were used for this book.

Another valuable feature of the book is the incorporation of many examples of educational technology devices, strategies, processes, resources, and online teaching techniques. The information is presented in a straightforward and practical manner. The topics in this book are useful for any educator who desires to learn principles and strategies for teaching and learning more effectively with technology.

Other features of this book include:

- practical examples of technology devices
- strategies for using technologies to enhance learning
- approaches to troubleshooting common technology equipment and devices
- strategies for maintaining and repairing basic computer and network problems
- a review of the history of technologies used for classroom and online settings

Lastly, this book also contains a rich source of educational technology references and websites for educators. The resources provide up-to-date information on technology and instruction across the various international and national standards on technology in education. This material should provide an essential foundation needed for an educator becoming a skilled user of technology for teaching and learning.

ONE

Introduction to Electronic Technologies

OBJECTIVES

At the conclusion of the chapter, the reader will be able to:

1. Understand the history of electricity, computer technologies, and electronic devices (ISTE 1, 3, 5).
2. Define *hardware* and *software,* and how they relate to each other in a computer (ISTE 1, 2, 3, 5).
3. Explain the most essential hardware components in a computer (ISTE 2, 3, 5).
4. Describe the basic and required software to operate a computer (ISTE 2, 3, 5).

INTRODUCTION

Computer and electronic technologies are extremely important for education. Over 90% of teachers in the United States have one or more computers located in the classroom (U.S. Department of Education, 2010). Almost all of these computers have access to the Internet. Many students are encouraged to bring iPads and laptops to classrooms. They use these electronic devices to take class notes, watch tutorials, complete homework, or take online exams.

Similarly, the U.S. Census Bureau (2013) recently reported that approximately 75% of households had a computer as compared to 8.2% in 1984. Additionally, 71% of households also had access to the Internet. Computer technologies are now essential parts of our daily lives. They are important tools for teaching and learning and exist everywhere, including schools and homes. This chapter provides an introduction to electronic and computer technologies starting with the history of electricity and the development of electronic devices. They have all contributed to modern-day technologies for teaching and learning.

HISTORY OF ELECTRICITY

Imagine a world without electricity. Imagine no computers, cars, lights, telephones, televisions, radios, refrigerators, medical operating rooms and equipment, microwave ovens, elevators, cell phones, and so on. The world depends on electricity. Most of the things we rely on for our everyday lives require electricity. This dependence is especially acute for those who use computers and other electronic technologies for work and play.

For educators, core traditional "technologies" like paper and pen don't require the constant use of electricity. But given a choice, most educators would prefer to use electricity-dependent modern technologies like laptops, video projectors, and wireless networks to support their work. How did we get from large, clunky mechanical calculators of the late 1800s to our wafer-thin handheld tablet computers today that can add, subtract, and play high-definition movies with stereo sound?

Technology has rapidly advanced since the 1940s with the invention of the world's first supercomputer, the Electronic Numerical Integrator and Computer (ENIAC). ENIAC required 1800 square feet of space and enormous amounts of electricity. The computational power of ENIAC can now fit in the palm of a person's hand.

To understand the development of electronic devices, it is important to start with the history of electrical generation. The electric incandescent light bulb was created because old flame-based lights from candles, lamps, and lanterns were dangerous. They were not very bright, generated smoke, and were only one accident away from burning down buildings.

Thomas Alva Edison did not invent the first incandescent light bulb, but his was the first commercially viable one. Coupled with a reliable electric generator and electricity distribution system, Edison's invention was ready for public use. The first commercial application of Edison's light bulb was on the steamship Columbia in 1879. The first home in New York City that had its own electric generator belonged to J. P. Morgan, on Fifth Avenue. Edison built a small power plant in the back yard and installed a power generator in the basement of the house. Edison used over 4,000 feet of wire to light up the Morgan residence.

To illuminate his light bulb, Edison developed an electric generator that produced direct current (DC). However, two of the major problems with the DC generator were that it required a lot of space and it produced a tremendous amount of rattling noise. Another major issue was that only a small number of residences were able to receive electricity because the DC power distribution was limited to the proximity of the generator. Even so, the Edison Illuminating Company received orders for generators to be installed that served both homes and industrial plants.

By 1882, the first street lamps were powered by the DC generators on Pearl Street in New York City. During this time, while Edison continued to improve the light bulb, Nicola Tesla, an assistant to Edison, developed a new form of a generator. This generator was able to produce a different type of electricity called *alternating current* (AC). Nikola Tesla presented this new AC concept to Edison, who rejected the idea. AC electricity was better for commercial applications because it was cheaper to generate and less expensive to distribute over long distances.

Tesla then approached George Westinghouse and presented his AC generator invention and patents. Westinghouse, upon consideration of Tesla's plan, agreed to pay Tesla royalties on the use of the AC patents. To build an electric power plant (a facility containing one or more electric generators), Westinghouse needed to secure financial backers. Westinghouse and Tesla collaborated and conducted demonstrations throughout the country selling AC electrical power.

Westinghouse in the late 1800s entered and won the competition against the Edison Illumination Company to light up the World's Fair of Chicago. At the World's Fair, 2,000 light bulbs were used to show the world that AC power was safe and reliable. This event led Westinghouse to secure a contract to build a commercial power plant at Niagara Falls. In 1895, this hydropower station, constructed by Niagara Falls Power Company, started generating AC electricity. Ironically, J. P. Morgan later bought the AC generator patents from Westinghouse.

AC power became the dominant source for consumer electricity. However, many electronic devices still needed DC to operate. As a result, power supplies were developed that converted AC to DC (see chapter 2). To this day, this conversion requirement affects users of electronic devices. Laptop users carry small plastic bricks in their bags, which provide this AC-to-DC conversion for their portable computers.

With the availability of this new power source, many electricity-based industrial machines were developed. Electrical machines and devices became the foundation of many industrial operations. They provided light, helped with repetitive mechanical tasks, supported communication, and later provided more sophisticated services requiring the manipulation of information.

HISTORY OF ELECTRONIC DEVICES

In 1904, John Fleming invented the vacuum tube diode (a two-terminal, thermionic emission valve), which marked the beginning of the electronics age. In 1906, Lee De Forest further developed this vacuum tube into a triode (three-terminal device) vacuum tube. A triode was a small device that could make weak electrical signals stronger (a process called *amplification*). The triode became one of the main components in the development of radios, televisions, radars, computers, and industrial control equipment.

The problem with vacuum tube triodes was that they burned out very fast. Replacing the tubes required many maintenance hours. Fortunately, in 1947 the vacuum tube problem was resolved with the invention of the transistor, a reliable semiconductor device that could replace the vacuum tube triode. William Shockley, Walter Brattain, and John Bardeen were successful in developing the transistor at the Bell Telephone Laboratories in Michigan.

Transistors were not only more reliable, they were also much smaller than vacuum tube triodes. Electronic device technology moved toward creating smaller and faster components. These small components led to more compact equipment designs. In 1958, the integrated circuit (IC) chip was invented, which became the basic foundation of the microprocessor (developed in 1971 by Intel Corporation). ICs and microprocessors are essential components in modern computers.

HISTORY OF COMPUTER TECHNOLOGIES

Originally, computers were thought of as devices to solve complex mathematical calculations without human error. During late 1930s, the first mechanical computer, the Z1, was invented and developed by Konrad Zuse. The Z1 contained many of the basic components of the modern computers such as a control unit, memory, and input and output devices. Programming was performed with punched cards or magnetic reel-to-reel tapes. The Z1 was completed in 1938 and destroyed during WWII when Berlin was bombarded by the Allies.

In 1937, Howard Aiken presented an idea to construct an electromechanical computer to International Business Machines (IBM). As a result, the Harvard Mark I was built. This computer was first used by the U.S. Navy from 1944 through 1959. The Harvard Mark I was also used by Jon von Neumann in the Manhattan Project. The objective of the Manhattan Project was to develop the atomic bomb.

During 1942 through 1946, the Manhattan Project was directed by scientists from the United States and assisted by experts from Canada and the United Kingdom. The University of Chicago, Oak Ridge National Lab, and Los Alamos National Lab were the main contributors to the project. Major General Leslie Groves of the U.S. Army Corps of Engineers was the director of the project at Los Alamos National Laboratory where the atomic bomb was designed. Physicist Robert Oppenheimer was the scientific director of the project.

In the 1940s, ENIAC was invented, which marked the beginning of the supercomputer era. ENIAC was the first general all-purpose electronic computer. Some of its unique features are listed in figure 1.1. Programming was performed by turning switches on and off. Jean Bartik, along with a team of five other women, was the original group of programmers.

One of the major problems of ENIAC was that the process of turning the computer on and off prematurely burned the vacuum tubes. Replacing them on a daily basis was time-consuming and costly. Computers required more efficient electronic devices than vacuum tubes to operate properly without excessive down time. ENIAC was used continuously

Components

10,000 capacitors
7,200 crystal diodes
5,000,000 hand soldered joints
1,500 relays
70,000 resistors
17,458 vacuum tubes

Power Usage
160 kilowatts

Cost, Weight, and Space

$500,000
25 tons
680 square feet

Figure 1.1. ENIAC's unique features.

from the 1940s to the mid-1950s until it was replaced by the Electronic Discrete Variable Automatic Computer (EDVAC).

The EDVAC's physical components included a magnetic tape reader or recorder, dual memory, and an oscilloscope. It was later updated in 1953 with a punch-card system and extra memory. For every eight hours of operation, the computer would crash for 20 hours as a result of burning or failure of the vacuum tubes. Fortunately, in 1947, the problem was solved by the invention of the semiconductor transistor. The transistor was smaller and more reliable than a vacuum tube triode (see chapter 2).

Using transistors, computers became significantly smaller and more efficient as they were operable continuously for long periods. As technology improved, so did the programming languages and computers. Likewise, auxiliary components such as the mouse, display monitor, and other peripheral equipment were developed. In 1958, Jack Kilby from Texas Instruments and Robert Noyce from Fairchild Semiconductors introduced and invented the IC. This IC was a chip containing numerous electronic components including transistors, resistors, capacitors, and diodes embedded in a silicon or germanium semiconductor material.

In 1964, chief architect Gene Amdahl introduced the IBM System/360 (S/360) under the chairmanship of Thomas Watson. The S/360 became the first computer able to perform scientific and commercial applications. This computer used an eight-bit (one byte) memory addressing system. It consisted of numerous transistors and IC chips.

In 1971, random-access memory (RAM) IC chips were developed, which led the way to the invention of microprocessors (see chapter 4). During this time, the floppy disk was also invented by Alan Shugart in collaboration with IBM. The floppy disk allowed significantly increased storage capabilities. Later, the IBM System/370 (S/370) was introduced, which was an improved version of the S/360. The S/370 computer had increased performance and was easier to operate.

In 1971, Federico Faggin, Ted Hoff, and Stanley Mazor invented the first microprocessor, the Intel 4004 Pentium chip. A microprocessor is an IC chip that has the functions of a computer's central processing unit (CPU) on that one chip. With 2,300 transistors etched into the silicon chip, the Intel 4004 microprocessor performed as many calculations per minute as the ENIAC (O'Regan, 2013). Today's microprocessor chips include billions of transistors. The continuing miniaturization of IC chips and microprocessors has allowed the possibility for significantly smaller computers.

In 1977, Apple Corporation developed one of the first successful personal home computers, the Apple II. IBM then launched its first personal computer (PC) in 1981. Both the Apple II and the IBM PC were small, inexpensive devices based on microprocessor technology. Prior to these products, computers were more of a novelty device, and they required some technical knowledge to actually set up and use. The Apple II and IBM PC were complete systems with all the hardware and software components ready to go in the box.

DEFINITION OF HARDWARE AND SOFTWARE

Hardware and software are the crucial components of every computer. *Hardware* is the mechanical, electrical, magnetic, or chemical components of the machine that can be physically touched. *Software* is the programming, or the instructions, that control the machine. Software tells the computer what, when, and how to do a specific task.

Hardware includes the semiconductor devices such as diodes, transistors, operational amplifiers, resistors, capacitors, inductors, and IC chips, which are all parts of the computer (see chapter 2). These electronic components serve specific purposes such as converting power from AC to DC. Functions of hardware include minimizing or suppressing the electrical noise, electronic switching, and amplification (making the signals larger). Hardware is also used to convert electrical signals from analog to digital and digital to analog.

The software is a set of machine-readable instructions that are provided to a computer. A computer program is a piece of software that does something specific. For example, a word processing program is an example of software. There are programming languages that enable people to write software (or code) for computers. Then programming language compilers or interpreters translate the code into something a computer can read and understand directly. The main piece of software on any computer is the operating system (OS). It governs the primary functioning of a computer and manages the running of other software.

UNDERSTANDING HARDWARE ESSENTIALS

All modern electronic devices have hardware associated with them. Typical hardware components include casing, the CPU, cooling devices, disks, memory modules, expansion cards, hard drives, motherboard, monitor, network interface card, power supply unit, and ports. Some of the essential hardware parts of a computer are shown in figure 1.2. The locations of these essential parts may differ from one computer to another.

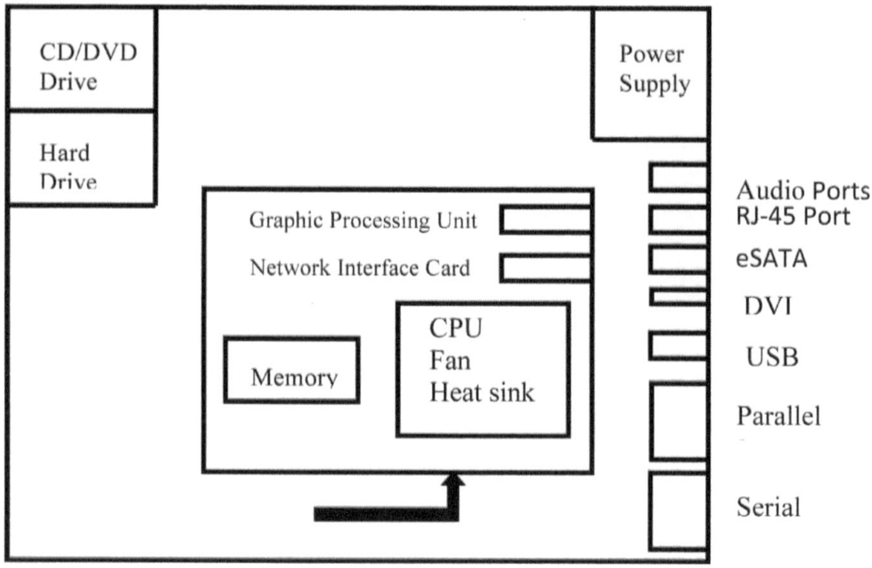

Figure 1.2. A computer's essential hardware parts.

Casing

The casing is the outer shell of the computer. It is made with nonmagnetic materials. All components of the computer are contained inside the casing. The outer part of the casing has an on–off switch, outlets for power supply, and several ports. Casings come in different sizes and shapes, with some as small as a cell phone and others as large as a tower.

Central Processing Unit

The CPU is an IC chip manufactured by a semiconductor company such as Intel Corporation. It is the brain of the computer that processes data and information through the software to produce a desired action. The CPU rapidly performs complex mathematical calculations. There are several parts of the CPU system; all of these parts are synchronized and controlled through the motherboard. The motherboard is the main circuit board that holds the majority of electrical circuits needed to operate the computer.

Cooling Devices

The CPUs and IC chips generate a lot of heat, which can damage the computer. Heat sinks, fans, heat pipes, and water coolers are used to eliminate heat from the CPU. Heat pipes are made out of copper and are connected to the CPU. The heat is taken away from the CPU by the heat pipes and distributed to a fan. As the fan turns, the heat travels through the fins and out of the CPU.

Disks

The compact disk (CD), digital video disk (DVD), and Blu-ray disk (BD) were invented to record and play audio sounds and videos. The original standard CD held up to eighty minutes of audio and 737 megabytes (MB) of data. The CD is read by a laser light. In 1982, the first CD was produced; it played Billy Joel's album *52nd Street*. In 1996, Toshiba Corporation (Japan) introduced the first DVD. A DVD can be double-sided, holds seven times more information than a CD, and stores 4.7 to 8.5 gigabytes (GB) of data.

The difference between a DVD and Blu-ray is the capacity of the disks. A Blu-ray disk's capacity enables it to record and play back high-definition video. The dual-layer Blu-ray produced in 2000 contains 25 to 50 GB of data. A triple-layer DVD can hold up to 100 GB of data, and a quadruple-layer DVD can hold in excess of 128 GB. They are all read by a 405-mm diode laser light.

Random-Access Memory

RAM is a form of computer memory that can be accessed by the computer at any time. There are two types of RAM: dynamic random-access memory (DRAM) and static random-access memory (SRAM). The DRAM data need to be periodically refreshed, while the SRAM data do not need to be refreshed. The SRAM is more reliable than DRAM and it can access information faster, but it is more expensive.

The DRAM chip is the basic storage unit for computers to store data. For example, when a user accesses a Microsoft Word application, the software associated with Word is stored in the DRAM temporarily. A typical DRAM has a size of 8 MB. Once the user completes working on the application and the computer is turned off, information on the DRAM is lost.

Single In-Line Memory Module

The single in-line memory module (SIMM) is a circuit board that has RAM chips soldered onto it along with a 30-pin connector mounted on the motherboard. A SIMM or several SIMMs can be connected to the motherboard of the computer. The SIMM has the memory capacity in excess of 8 MB.

Dual In-Line Memory Module

With increased speed, more data per second (bandwidth) is achievable. More RAM memory is needed to store large amounts of data in a given amount of time. The dual in-line memory module (DIMM) is developed to meet the demands of technology. The DIMM is a circuit board that typically has eight RAM chips soldered onto it with a 168- or 184-pin connector mounted on the board. The DIMM has the following sizes: 8, 18, 32, 64, 128, 256, and 512 MB, 1 GB, and so on. More RAM chips are embedded to obtain a larger DIMM. Several DIMMs can be connected to the motherboard to create a 2-GB or larger RAM.

Dual-Voltage Selector

A dual-voltage selector switch is used to turn on a power supply source to 110 or 220 volts. Depending on the standard voltage supply level at different countries, a switch should be set to 110 or 220 volts. In the United States the standard voltage is 110 volts. If the selector switch is not set correctly to the correct voltage, the computer may be damaged or not operate properly.

Expansion Cards

Expansion cards, also known as *adaptor cards,* are used to extend the capabilities of the motherboard of the computer. Expansion cards are placed into slots on the motherboard to create the ports necessary to perform additional functions for the computer. Examples of expansion cards are sound, graphics, and network interface cards.

Graphic Processing Unit

The graphic processing unit (GPU) is a card with just one purpose: create images and computer graphics. The GPU is also called a *visual processing unit* (VPU). It is an embedded system, which means it is included on the motherboard. GPU is used as a video card if used in mobile devices.

Hard Drive and External Drive

The hard disk drive (HDD) is used to permanently store digital data (figure 1.3). A computer may contain more than one hard drive. An external hard drive is also available, which provides extra storage. An

Figure 1.3. Hard disk drive.

external hard drive has a storage capacity in terabytes (TB); 1 TB is equal to approximately 1,000,000,000,000 bytes. Some old and modern types of external drives are tape, floppy disk, CD, DVD, and Blu-ray drives. A hard drive or external drive is connected to the computer through a universal serial bus (USB) port.

Form Factor

The form factor of a computer describes the configuration and size of the motherboard, casing, and power supply. The Advanced Technology eXtended (ATX) and Micro ATX are examples of the form factors used for the desktop computers. An ATX motherboard contains more than five expansion cards. The Micro ATX motherboard is smaller than the ATX motherboard. The Micro ATX contains up to four expansion slots. The cost of a Micro ATX computer is less than an ATX computer.

Motherboard

The motherboard holds the CPU and the supporting IC chips. The daughterboard supports the gate drivers, sensors, and power metal-oxide semiconductor field-effect transistors (MOSFETs). Through millions of MOSFET IC chips, the computer performs basic switching functions, which are needed for computer operations. Both motherboards and daughterboards are connected to the computer ports by cables and plugs.

Monitor

The monitor allows data to be viewed on a screen. It generally connects to the computer, smart phone, iPhone, iPad, router, switch, and other network devices. With the advancement of technology, the monitor has advanced from a high-definition multimedia interface (HDMI) and video graphics array (VGA) to a wireless monitor on TV screens, eyeglasses, and wristwatches. The modern monitor is a glass touch-screen on which data can be moved and manipulated.

Network Interface Card

The network interface card (NIC) is an expansion card that provides the means through which a computer communicates with a computer network. When a user tries to access a website, the information is transmitted from the motherboard to the NIC card or wireless adapter. The NIC card in a desktop computer has an RJ-45 connecter, which connects to an Ethernet cable. This cable connects to the network device such as a hub, switch, or router, which in turn accesses the Internet (see chapter 4) to get information from the target website.

Each computer has a unique identification number called the *media access control* (MAC) address, which is stored in the NIC. When the data are received by another network from the transmitting computer, the network switch looks at its MAC address table. After finding the MAC address of the destination computer on the table, the switch transmits the information to the appropriate computer.

Power Supply Unit

The power supply unit (PSU) converts an AC voltage source to a DC voltage supply. Through an electrical cable, the AC source of 110 volts from the wall plug is connected to the computer's DC power supply. Typical voltages of the DC power supplies are 3.3, 5, and 12 volts. The digital circuits use 3.3 and 5 volts; the motors for the fans and the disk drives use 12 volts. The power supplies are rated in watts (see chapter 2).

Port and Port Types

A port is a receptacle or jack used to connect a computer to peripheral equipment such as a mouse or printer. Computers and electronic devices have different ports for different purposes. For a smart phone or a tablet there is some type of input device or screen on the casing that is sensitive to touch, known as a *touch screen.* The following are typical ports found in a desktop computer:

- An audio port is a receptacle or jack where a computer can be connected to audio devices such as speakers, headphones, or microphones.
- An external serial advanced technology attachment (eSATA) port typically has a high-speed FireWire connector and an external hard drive connector.
- A display port is used to transmit digital video and audio signals.
- A digital video interface (DVI) port is used to transmit digital video signals. The connector, called a *DVI-A,* has two screws at each end to ensure a secure connection, but it only transmits analog videos. The DVI-I connector is used digitally only and it is universal.
- An Institute of Electrical and Electronics Engineers (IEEE) 1394 port is used for multimedia devices that require high speeds.
- An HDMI port is used only to transmit digital video and audio signals.
- A network port, also known as an *Ethernet port* or *RJ-45 port,* is used to connect the computer to the network.
- The USB port is one of the most common types of ports used to connect or charge a multitude of electronic devices.

The USB ports are located along the side of the computer and are used to attach external devices such as printers and keyboards, as well as download data into USB flash drives. The USB ports can also be used to charge cell phones or other devices like tablets. Information is transmitted fast and one port can support several devices with an extension connection.

UNDERSTANDING SOFTWARE ESSENTIALS

Software runs the CPU, the brain of a computer. Without software, a computer would not be able to function. The different types of software on a computer include embedded software, OS software, device driver software, firmware, and server software.

Computers function by processing information in a binary form (ones and zeros), but people cannot efficiently read or write in binary code.

Programs called *compilers* translate instructions written in computer languages that people can understand into binary code that a computer can understand. In 1951, the first compiler program invented by Grace Hopper, turned data and commands into binary ones and zeros. Numerous computer languages have developed over time since then, including Fortran, BASIC, Pascal, C, C++, JavaScript, ASP.NET, Perl, and Python.

Embedded Software and Operating System Software

The embedded software is stored within the CPU. It has specific functions and it is interrelated to the operation of the whole system. Removal of the embedded software might cause a failure in another part of the computer. The OS software manages the function of all other software on a computer. Within the OS software there is a time-sharing system, which allows a computer to maximize efficient use of the system resources to perform the required tasks.

Each OS is designed and developed to work with a specific group of electronic devices. Windows-based computers and Macintosh computers have different OSs. Android smartphones and the iPhone have different OSs. Chapter 5 discusses these issues in greater detail.

Device Driver Software

The device driver software enables a computer to communicate with and control other devices. It is an essential piece of software that enables the use of a vast number of interesting and useful internal and external devices. The use of keyboards, mice, and monitors are made possible by device driver software.

Firmware

Firmware is the embedded programmable software and hardware intended for specific devices. Examples of specific devices that have firmware are digital watches, digital cameras, smart phones, and remote controls for televisions. Firmware contains a memory chip that controls the device. Firmware can be removed or changed from the device only in rare circumstances. Replacing a device that does not work is usually a better option than trying to replace its firmware.

Server Software

Servers are computers dedicated to providing specific services like file storage, web services, print services, and so on. These computers are usually loaded with special software called server software. Application, database, file, game, mail, printer, and web are examples of server-based services.

SUMMARY

The invention of practical electrical devices like light bulbs, paired with the development of dependable electric generation and distribution systems, led to the early adoption and use of electricity and electrical machines. Further development led to the creation of numerous electronic components and devices such as vacuum tubes, diodes, transistors, IC chips, and microprocessors. Electronic devices and the early supercomputer led the way to current mini- and microcomputers that can be as small as a wristwatch.

During the 1930s, the first mechanical computer was invented by Konrad Zuse and was called the Z1. Howard Aiken presented the idea to construct a new electromechanical computer to IBM in 1937. As a result, the Harvard Mark I was built and it was first used by the U.S. Navy between 1944 and 1959.

Today, sophisticated computers exist that perform complex operations. Most computers have physical internal mechanical, electrical, magnetic, and chemical components called *hardware*. Hardware includes semiconductor devices such as diodes, transistors, operational amplifiers, resistors, capacitors, inductors, and integrated circuit chips, which are all parts of the computer. All these electronic components serve specific purposes such a converting power from AC to DC, minimizing or suppressing the electrical noise, electronic switching, and amplification.

Software is the programming or the code that tells the computer what, when, and how to do a specific task. The code is written in computer languages that people can understand, and is then translated by a compiler or interpreter into a binary language that computers can understand. An OS is the main software that controls and manages the overall functioning of a computer. Through the OS, a computer is able to time, coordinate, and control the operation of the keyboard, mouse, printer, and other peripheral devices.

CASE STUDY

You have been asked to give a presentation on the history of computer technology development. Prepare an outline of the chronological events and inventions that have significantly contributed to the advancement of computers. Also include some of the common hardware and software components of a typical computer. Draw a diagram of the internal components of the computer and provide an explanation of how it operates.

EXERCISES AND DISCUSSION QUESTIONS

1. List and describe the software applications and specific functions of the computer. Include the typical components needed to support software applications.
2. Describe how technology has contributed to the evolution of education.
3. Identify some of the most prominent people who have contributed to computer evolution and how they have influenced other people. Include examples of the major contributions and effects on society and education.

REFERENCES

Gosling, F. G. (2005). *The Manhattan project: Making the atomic bomb.* Retrieved from http://www.atomicarchive.com/History/mp/index.shtml

O'Regan, G. (2013). *Giants of computing: A compendium of select, pivotal pioneers.* London: Springer-Verlag.

U.S. Census Bureau. (2013). *Computer and internet use in the United States.* Retrieved from http://www.census.gov/prod/2013pubs/p20-569.pdf

U.S. Department of Education. (2010). *Teachers' use of educational technology in U.S. public schools: 2009.* Retrieved from http://nces.ed.gov/pubs2010/2010040.pdf

Two

Electronics and Technology

OBJECTIVES

At the conclusion of the chapter, readers will be able to:

1. Understand fundamentals of electricity and electronics (ISTE 1, 2; National Council for Accreditation of Teacher Education [NCATE] 2, 3).
2. Describe basic electronic components (ISTE 3, 4; NCATE 3).
3. Explain the basic theory of technology devices (ISTE 3, 4; NCATE 3).
4. Understand basic safety, maintenance, and troubleshooting of educational technology (ISTE 3, 4, 5; NCATE 3, 4).

FUNDAMENTALS OF ELECTRICITY AND ELECTRONICS

How does a computer work? What happens when you apply power to a Smart Board? Why is a power strip necessary? How do computer monitors work? Having a basic understanding of electricity and electronics can help you become a more effective technology educator in operating, maintaining, and troubleshooting educational devices.

To understand basic electricity and electronics you must first have knowledge of the *structure of matter*. All matter, such as people, equipment, materials, and the earth, is made up of very small particles called *atoms*. The atom is considered the smallest particle that can be condensed and still be considered an element. The structure of the atom consists of an inner core called the *nucleus*. The nucleus contains positive particles called *protons* and neutral particles called *neutrons*.

Revolving around the nucleus are tiny, nearly weightless negative particles called *electrons*. The mass of the electron is considered nearly 2,000 times less than the proton. The electrons that revolve in the outer shell of an atom are called *valence electrons*. Most atoms contain the same number of protons and electrons and are said to be balanced.

For example, the most basic atom is called *hydrogen*. A hydrogen atom has one proton particle, which has a positive charge. It also has one electron, which surrounds the nucleus of the atom. Likewise, the hydrogen atom has a neutron that contains a neutral charge and is neither positive nor negative. Hydrogen is considered a chemical element and has an atomic number 1. It is the lightest element on the periodic table and is colorless and odorless.

Another example of an atom is *carbon*. This atom contains six protons, six electrons, and six neutrons. The electrons are said to orbit the nucleus. The first orbit contains two electrons and the second orbit contains the remaining four electrons, which revolve around the nucleus. The carbon atom is an abundant element and is present in all life forms. It is also used in electronics as a resistance material for making resistors and other components.

Figure 2.1 illustrates an example of a carbon atom containing six protons, six neutrons, and six electrons. If an atom contains more or fewer electrons than protons, it is said to be *ionized*. These extra or missing electrons are the results of a sharing process called *ionization*. Also, notice the

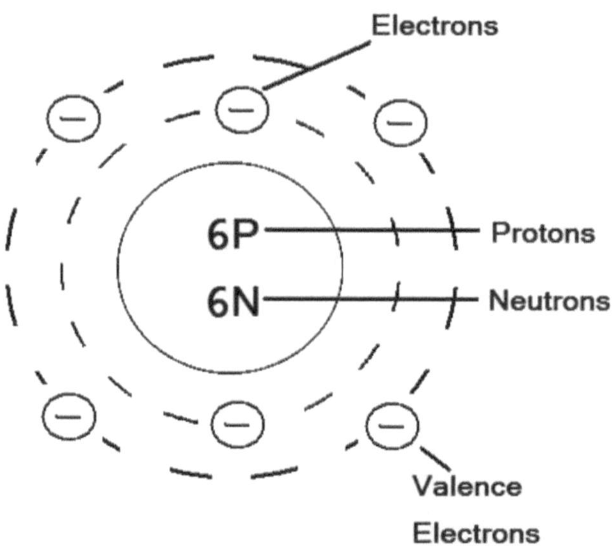

Figure 2.1. Example of carbon atom and elements.

Term	Definition	Measurement	Symbol
Voltage	The force (EMF), or pressure, of electrons flowing in a circuit	Volts	E or V
Amperage	Amount (current) of electrons flowing in a circuit	Amperes	I
Resistance	Opposition to electron flow in a circuit	Ohms	R or Ω
Inductance Reactance	Opposition to electron flow in a circuit because of inductors	Ohms	XL
Capacitance Reactance	Opposition to electron flow in a circuit because of capacitors	Ohms	Xc
Impedance	Opposition to electron flow due to all reactance and resistances	Ohms	Z

Figure 2.2. Electrical terminology, measurements, and symbols.

four valence electrons in figure 2.1 that are often referred to as "spinning" around the outer shell. When the electrons flow in a circuit, this is called *electricity*.

The three basic units of electricity are *voltage, amperage,* and *resistance*. *Voltage* can be defined as the electromotive force (EMF) or pressure of electrons flowing in a circuit (figure 2.2). *Amperage* can be defined as the quantity or the amount of the electrons flowing in a circuit. Lastly, *resistance* can be defined as the opposition to the electron flow in a circuit.

If you visualize a typical expressway, the speed of the vehicles can be considered the voltage. The number of cars traveling on the expressway can be called the amperage. The resistance to the vehicles would be anything that hinders the movement of the vehicles such as toll gates, construction areas, and stop signs. Therefore, at any given time, the voltage, amperage, and resistance in a circuit can vary depending on the circuit conditions and loads (devices that consume electrical power).

Another way to explain electricity is with the analogy of a garden water hose. If the water freely flows out of the hose, the amount of the water flowing can be considered the amperage. How fast the water travels through the hose is considered voltage. If you place your finger on the end of the hose and the water sprays out forcibly, this can be called *high voltage*. The flow of the water is analogous to the flow of electrons in an electrical circuit.

If a large quantity of water is flowing, but without much force, this can be considered high amperage. The voltage in this case would be low. The actual valve, or spigot, that regulates the amount of water flow can be called the *resistor*. If the valve is closed completely off, the flow of water (i.e., electricity) stops. This is similar to shutting off a switch in your home.

The measurement of voltage is expressed in volts and can be calculated by using a voltmeter. The symbols for voltage are the letters *V* (voltage) or *E* (EMF). Amperage is measured using an ammeter and is measured in amperes (or amps). The symbol for amperage is the letter "*I*." Another name for amperage is *current*. Resistance is expressed in ohms and is measured using an ohmmeter. The symbol for resistance is the letter *R* or the Greek omega sign (Ω).

When you turn on a technology device such as a computer, voltage flows to the unit, typically 115 to 130 volts (the average is 120 volts). The amperage is determined by the amount of electrical energy drawn by the device. The resistance is the compilation of the wires and components in the circuits. Resistance can only be measured when the power is off in the circuit.

Electrical power is the rate of electrical energy and is measured in watts (one joule per second). The formula for determining electrical power is voltage multiplied times amperage ($P = E \times I$). Electric power is usually sold in kilowatt hours. *Reactance* is the resistance caused by inductors (XL) or capacitors (XC). The sum total of all reactance and resistance is called *impedance* (Z).

The relationship of voltage, amperage, and resistance can be explained using Ohm's Law. This theory states that voltage is equal to current multiplied by resistance ($E = I \times R$). Amperage is calculated by dividing resistance into voltage, and resistance is determined by dividing the amperage into voltage. This is the mathematical equation in calculating these three units of electricity.

Another common term in electronics is *conductivity*, which is a measure of a material's ability to conduct electricity. Materials vary in their ability to conduct electricity. For example, materials like copper, silver, and gold that allow electrons to flow easily are called *conductors*. Other materials, like rubber and glass that have a great amount of resistance and do not allow the free movement of electrons are called *insulators*.

Some materials are called *semiconductors* because their conductivity lies somewhere in between an insulator and a conductor. Materials like silicon and germanium are considered semiconductors because they allow free electrons to flow but are not good conductors or insulators. Semiconductors are the fundamental materials that are used to create transistors—the backbone of electronic circuitry.

Another common term used in electronic technology is *power*. Power is described as the rate of doing work in electrical circuits and it is calculated by multiplying the voltage times the amperage ($P = V \times I$). When a person describes the power of a technology device, it represents the product of the voltage and the amperage being drawn. The unit of measurement of electrical power is called the *watt.*

The *watt* is the amount of power converted when one amp of current flows with one volt pressure. Electric utility companies install watt meters to determine the amount of power being used to calculate the cost (i.e., kilowatt hours). Therefore, when referring to the term *power,* remember that it is essentially a combination of the amount of voltage and amperage the electronic device is using. Technology devices that tend to use a lot of power are smart televisions, air conditioners, and space heaters. Electronic devices that do not use much power are light-emitting diodes (LEDs), fluorescent lights, document cameras, radios, and printers.

There are three fundamental kinds of electricity: alternating current (AC), direct current (DC), and static electricity. AC is a special type of electricity commonly used to power residential and commercial facilities and equipment. This electricity is created by an AC generator in an electrical power plant. The generator produces power by magnetism. To understand AC, you must first understand the theory of the magnet.

You may recall in your past science courses that the word *magnetism* itself gets its name from the ancient Greeks who first experimented with pieces of iron ore called *magnetite.* In their experiments they found that these pieces of magnetic ore are sometimes attracted each other and so they called this amazing phenomenon *magnetism.*

Later, ancient European sailors used pieces of magnetite to form a compass that would help guide them in their sea journeys. They called this magnetic device a *load stone.* Today, magnets have many uses and can be found in such devices as smart televisions, projectors, computers, circuit breakers, and power strips.

All magnets have two poles: a north pole and a south pole. Surrounding a magnet is an invisible magnetic field called a *magnetic flux.* Artificial magnets can be produced by rubbing an iron rod with a silk cloth. Permanent magnets are usually made of high carbon steel and last longer than temporary magnets. Also, strong permanent magnets sometimes are made up of alloy materials called *alnico,* which is chiefly composed of aluminum, nickel, and cobalt.

Some magnets can be demagnetized by heating or striking the magnet. When a magnetized bar contains particles that align in an orderly fashion, it is said to be *magnetized.* The earth is one enormous magnet in which the magnetic north is located near the geographic North Pole and the magnetic south is located near the geographic South Pole. Like magnets repel each other and unlike poles attract each other.

The basis of AC is *electromagnetism.* Electromagnetism can be produced by electric current flowing through a conductor by a magnet. Wrapping insulated wires around an iron bar with the two ends of the wire connected to an electrical source is called an *electromagnet.* When the current is reversed, the electromagnet will reverse the polarity in the iron bar.

A simple definition of the alternating generator is a device that contains many turns of wire in a rotating armature surrounded by magnetic coils that produces electricity. When a turbine turns the armature, electricity is produced (figure 2.3). The AC generator armature rotates one complete revolution (360 degrees) and produces a complete AC sine wave. This current flows in one direction from 0 to 180 degrees during the positive part and then flows in the opposite direction during the last 180-degree negative half-cycle. In the United States, there are 60 cycles per second, or hertz (Hz).

The trick to producing AC is to spin the turbine that turns the armature to create electrical energy. The turbine can be spun with high-pressure steam from boiling water. The water can be boiled using natural gas, petroleum, or nuclear fuel rods. Turbines can also be spun through the use of renewable-energy devices such as hydroelectric water dams or wind turbine aerodynamic blades. For example, the wind turbine converts kinetic wind energy into electrical energy.

DC can be produced by a DC generator or by a battery. DC does not alternate cycles from positive to negative, but rather flows directly from negative to positive through the circuit. AC and DC power are critical to the operation of technology devices. The power that flows to a computer or other device is generally AC. This power is then rectified into a low-voltage DC to operate the device.

Static electricity is referred to as "electricity at rest." It is said to be neither negative nor positive. A common example of static electricity is the a slight shock experienced when touching an electronic device such as a television while walking across a carpeted floor. Lightning is another example of static electricity. It is produced when clouds develop a charge that is transmitted to earth.

Static electricity, also called *electrostaticity,* can cause significant problems to technology devices because it can produce spontaneous shocks that can harm or destroy the components in the circuit. Also, most semiconductor components in a technology device are sensitive to electrosta-

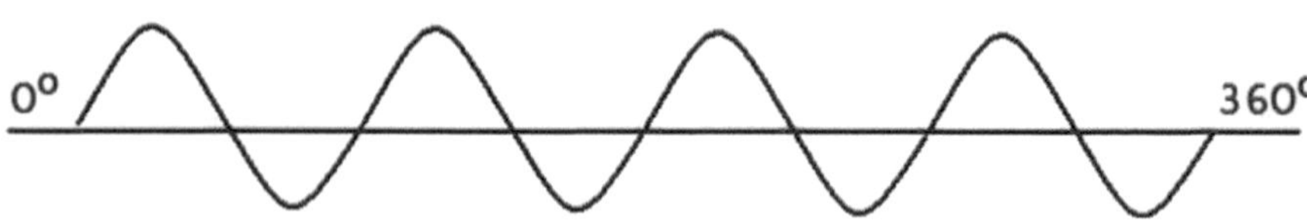

Figure 2.3. Example of alternating current sign wave.

ticity. Caution should be taken to ensure that these sensitive devices are not exposed to static electricity.

For example, when installing a semiconductor component such as a random-access memory (RAM) semiconductor chip, make sure to avoid any electrostatic charges. This can be accomplished by wearing a grounding strap that connects your body to earth ground. This helps prevent electrostatic buildup in your body and minimizes damage to the component. Also, the use of antistatic mats on the floor and other antistatic products can help eliminate electrostatic harm to technology equipment.

It is best not to use technology equipment and devices on a carpet because this can produce electrostatic charges more easily than hardwood flooring. Another popular antistatic device is the use of a wrist strap and ground bracelet. The use of these devices keeps you grounded and prevents the development of electrostaticity. The operation of these devices creates an avenue for voltage charges to leak through your body to the earth ground and prevent static buildup.

Also, make sure that there are no hazardous combustible, flammable, or explosive materials around the equipment because electrostaticity can build up and create a fire. Anytime an electronic module or other integrated circuit device is handled, damage can be produced even with minimal voltage or movement. Moreover, damage can occur by excessive vibration and contamination such as dust, dirt, and liquids.

It is also important to understand the different types of circuit connections. There are three basic electric circuit connections in which electrical devices can be connected: series, parallel, and series-parallel. The performance of the technology device will vary depending on the type of circuit combination.

In a *series circuit* the electricity has only one path available. For example, if three lamps and a battery are connected in series, the source voltage is divided among all three lamps. Each lamp will receive the same voltage, and if one lamp burns out, the entire circuit will cease to operate. In a series circuit, the voltage is the total of the voltage drops and is equal to the voltage applied to the circuit. Likewise, the total resistance of a series circuit is the sum of the resistances of the lamps. The amperage is always the same across each lamp in the circuit.

An example of a series circuit is a set of cheap Christmas tree light bulbs. To keep costs low, this string of light bulbs is connected in a series circuit. Less wire is needed to produce a series circuit than a parallel circuit. Therefore, if one bulb goes bad, the entire Christmas light string goes off. The defective bulb must be replaced for all the light bulbs to work.

In a *parallel circuit* all lamps receive the same amount of voltage, unlike the series circuit. For example, if three lamps are connected to a battery, all three lamps receive the same amount of voltage. If one lamp burns out, the other lamps will remain lit and unaffected by the one burnt-out lamp. This is similar to the devices that are plugged into residential electrical outlets. Each light bulb, in essence, is independent of the others.

Typical parallel circuits are sometimes called *shunt circuits* and can be found in the wiring of homes, commercial buildings, and electronic devices. In parallel circuits the amperage varies depending on the amount of current drawn by each of the loads. Therefore, the total amperage is the sum of all the amperages drawn by the loads. The total resistance is calculated by a mathematical formula of $1/RT = 1/R1 + 1/R2 + 1/R3$.

The last circuit is called the *series-parallel circuit* (figure 2.4). In this circuit, the source voltage is divided among the lamp in series and the two lamps in parallel. For example, if the first lamp draws 6 volts, then the second and third lamps draw 6 volts (the second lamp receives 3 volts and the third lamp receives 3 volts). If the first lamp in the series burns out, the circuit is broken and the other two lamps will also go off.

However, in this circuit if either the second or third lamp burns out, the circuit will not be broken and the remaining two lamps will remain lit. Also, if both lamps two and three burn out, the circuit will be broken and the first lamp will also go out. The combinations of these circuits are very common in technology devices.

Every technology educator should have a very basic understanding of circuit faults. A *circuit fault* is an electronic breakdown in which the device ceases to operate or operates inefficiently. Circuit faults can be caused by many factors such as overuse, natural deterioration, mechanical failure, moisture, dirt and contaminants, poor installation, and abnormal or excessive use.

There are four common types of circuit faults: short circuit, open circuit, ground circuit, and mechanical fault. A *short circuit* is created when the

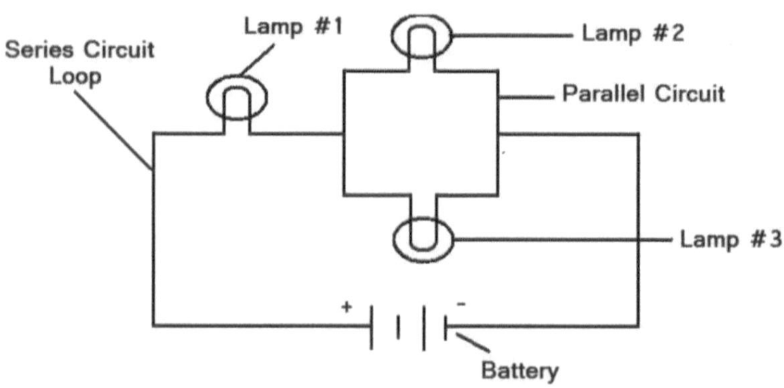

Figure 2.4. Example of a series-parallel circuit.

electricity takes a direct path across the circuit and there is (near) zero resistance. This can be caused by wires touching each other or insulation breakdown where an indirect path is created. Short circuits can be dangerous and typically will trip the circuit breaker or blow a fuse. The equipment will cease to operate until the short can be identified and corrected.

An *open circuit* is different than a short circuit. The resistance in an open circuit is nearly infinite. An example of an open circuit occurs when a wire is broken or cut open and the current path is prevented. In this case the device will not operate. An open circuit typically will not trip a circuit breaker or blow a fuse, but simply will not operate. This is equivalent to the device not being plugged into the power outlet or the power button not being engaged.

A *ground fault* can be a serious threat to not only the technology device but also the operator. This fault is created when part of the electrical current flowing into the device is directed to the frame. Ground faults can be created because of poor insulation, breakdown of insulation, pinched wires, misplaced components, and broken wires that come in contact with the frame of the device.

For example, a common ground fault can occur when the internal circuit wires are pinched when the operator is replacing the metal cover of a device (e.g., computer). In this situation, part of the current can flow through the device, and possibly through the operator, to earth ground. In this situation, the operator could become part of electrical circuit and experience electrical shock or even death.

Ground faults often cause a device to function poorly or cease operation. Ground faults can be hard to diagnose and require meticulous analysis and testing of the circuit boards and components. Once the problem has been identified, corrective action then needs to be taken. Qualified, authorized technicians should service any technology device with electronic faults.

The last common circuit problem is called the *mechanical fault*. These can be caused by excessive wear, abuse, vibration, or friction where the physical part of the device causes a breakdown. A damaged chassis or a defective pushbutton are examples. Mechanical faults can also cause noisy operation, abnormal operation, and circuit failure.

There are a number of safety considerations every educator needs to understand when operating technology equipment. No matter how competent you feel as a technology educator in using equipment, you must respect the power of electricity and follow proper safety guidelines. Electricity can be very unpredictable and, theoretically speaking, cannot be seen, felt, smelled, or heard—although its results can be experienced.

Therefore, always respect electrical power. Electricity can have damaging effects to the body. As little as 200 milliamperes (mA) of current applied to a person's heart can cause muscles to involuntarily contract and cause paralysis, breathing disruption, ventricular fibrillation, and even death. You should always follow basic safety guidelines when operating equipment:

1. Do not use spray chemicals near electronic devices.
2. Avoid all drinks, moisture, and fluids near technology devices.
3. Never attempt to service a technology device unless professionally authorized.
4. Shut the electrical power off when moving technology equipment.
5. Avoid poor connections and wires that are cluttered or excessively long.
6. Take special caution to reduce or eliminate electrostaticity near technology devices.
7. Read the set-up instructions to ensure that the proper voltage is supplied to the device.
8. Read the entire operating manual that accompanies a technology device to ensure proper maintenance, safety, and operation.

The responsible technology educator is always on the lookout for unusual noises, smells, and visual defects. These can give you a signal that something is wrong. Also, practicing proper operation and maintenance of technology equipment can help prevent common circuit faults and contribute to longer lasting electronic equipment.

UNDERSTANDING ELECTRICAL COMPONENTS

To be a good technology educator, you do not need to be an electrical engineer, but having a basic understanding of how the technology operates can help you in maintaining, troubleshooting, and using the equipment. Most technology devices come with an operating manual that includes basic circuitry, troubleshooting, schematics, and symbols. Some of the most common electronic components are displayed in figure 2.5.

Learning the electronic symbols is similar to learning another language. Combinations of these symbols allow the electronic engineer to create circuits that are the building blocks of all technology devices. A *resistor* is a common passive electronic component that restricts the amount of current flow in a circuit. Some resistors have fixed resistances and are little affected by temperature. Resistors are made from a variety of materials such as carbon, wire film, metal, and foil.

Variable resistors are often called *potentiometers* or *rheostats*. They provide a variable resistance to control current flow such as a light dimmer.

Component	Symbol	Application
Fixed Resistor		Restricts current flow through resistance material.
Variable Resistor (potentiometer)	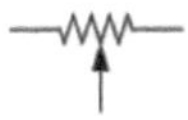	Provides a variable resistance and restricts current flow.
Fixed Capacitor		Stores electrical energy for charging and signal filtering (e.g. pass high-frequencies, block low).
Variable Capacitor		Acts as a variable condenser for charging and signal filtering.
Battery		Contains two or more cells to supply electrical energy.
Diode		Acts as a one-way gate for current flow in one direction and blocks flow in the other direction.
Transistor (npn)	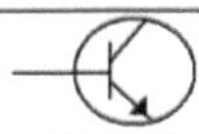	Provides switching operations and amplification and contains a base, emitter and collector (pnp or npn transistor).
Transistor (pnp)	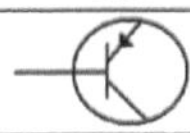	
Transformer (iron core)		Transfers electrical energy between two circuits such as step up or step down voltages.
Coil or inductor		Produces high voltage pulses and used for signal filtering (e.g., pass low frequencies, block high frequencies).

Figure 2.5. Examples of electric components, symbols, and application.

Adjustable resistors are similar to a variable resistor and contain several points of contact where the resistance is at a predetermined level for use in electronic circuits. Other more exotic resistors are made from tantalum, alloys, or resins that are used in special electronic applications.

Capacitors, also known as *condensers,* are passive electrical components that store electricity. They are constructed by assembling two conductors, called *plates,* separated by an insulating *dielectric* material. They are made from a variety of materials such as ceramic, plastic, paper, mica, film, and glass. Capacitors are used for several applications such as helping start electric motors, blocking DC voltage, and filtering signals. For example, capacitors can pass high-frequency signals, but restrict low-frequency signals.

The unit of measurement of the capacitor is the *farad,* which is equal to 1 coulomb per volt. When electricity is applied to a capacitor, an electrical field is produced across the dielectric insulator, which produces a charge on the plates. One plate develops a positive charge and the other a negative charge. Capacitors, like resistors, can be fixed or variable. Some capacitors can be checked by using an ohmmeter or capacitor checker. Capacitors, like most components, can develop shorts or grounds, or can lose its capacitance storage ability.

Inductors are passive electronic components and sometimes called *coils* or *reactors*. Similar to a capacitor, the inductor can temporarily store electrical energy through the process called *induction* (a magnetic field caused by current passing through a coil of wire). The unit of measurement of inductance is the *Henry*. Inductors are made from insulated copper wires and other materials. They are used to block the flow of AC and passes DC. They are used in many applications such as transformers and signal filtering.

A *transformer* is a device that transfers electrical energy between two inductors through the process of induction. When current passes through the first inductor, a magnetic flux is produced that electromagnetically transfers electrical energy to the other inductor. Transformers have a wide range of applications in technology devices and are typically used to step-up and step-down voltages. They can be used in extremely large, high-voltage distribution systems and in tiny computer power supplies.

One of the most useful electronic active components is the *transistor.* The transistor is a semiconductor and is used for logic switching and amplification such as in a computer or smart television. The construction of a transistor begins with a crystal material of silicon or germanium. Silicon has an atomic number 14 with four valence electrons and germanium has an atomic number of 32, also with four valence electrons.

The first step in constructing a transistor is to form a p-type material by integrating an impurity of gallium or indium, called a *trivalent*. A trivalent has only three valence electrons. Therefore, when the trivalent is combined with the crystal material, one valence electron is left unfilled. This unfilled gap is called a *hole* and takes a positive charge, which forms the p-type material.

The next step is to create an n-type material. To form it, an impurity such as arsenic or antimony is integrated. These materials are called an *acceptor impurity* because they contain five valence electrons that combine with the four valence electrons, adding one extra electron. This extra donor electron creates a negative charge, called a *pentavalent*.

When three materials are then constructed in an npn or pnp combination, a transistor is formed. The transistor has three parts called the *emitter,* the *base,* and the *collector*. The quality of some transistors can be checked using an ohmmeter. Resistance between the emitter and base connectors should measure at infinite (very high) resistance in one direction and (near) zero resistance in the other direction. This is also true when measuring the resistance between the collector and base. If infinite resistance is obtained in both directions, the transistor is probably open. And if zero resistance is obtained in both directions, it is probably shorted.

Transistors have many purposes, and there are many different types of transistors. One type is the field effect transistor, which is a special transistor used in high-frequency communications. The metal-oxide-semiconductor-field-effect transistor is used for high-input impedance (resistance) operations. Another popular type of transistor is the LED, which is a sophisticated electronic component that produces illumination.

The diode is an active device that rectifies AC to DC. It is formed by combining p and n materials. The diode allows current to pass in one direction, called *forward bias,* but blocks current in the other direction, called *reverse bias*. The positive side of the diode is called the *anode* and the negative side the *cathode*. The peak inverse rating of the diode indicates the amount of current it will prevent from flowing when reversed biased without leaking or destroying the diode. Therefore, two diodes back-to-back form a transistor.

Diodes can be checked using an ohmmeter or diode checker. A good diode measures resistance in one direction, but not in the other direction. If resistance is measured in both directions (i.e., zero resistance) the diode is probably shorted. If resistance is not measured in both directions (i.e., infinite resistance), it is probably open.

ELECTRONIC TECHNOLOGY APPLICATIONS

How do these components form circuits, products, and devices? The combinations of these components form some amazing technology. To understand the operation of a typical device, start by tracing the power from an electrical outlet box to a computer. Starting at the power outlet, often called a *duplex outlet,* there is approximately 120 AC voltage.

Next, a power strip is plugged into the duplex outlet. The power strip performs some or all of the following functions:

1. Expansion of outlets to provide power to devices such as printers, DVD players, computers, smart televisions, computer monitors, and projectors
2. Motion detectors that contain sensors for switching off devices when not in use
3. Surge protectors and circuit breakers to interrupt electrical flow in case of power overload and short circuits.

4. Electrical lightning surge protectors in the event of excessive power surges
5. Peak protectors that contain high-speed switches that momentarily limit peak voltages
6. Inductor-capacitor networks to protect equipment from high voltage spikes from the main circuit
7. Overload protection to automatically shut off devices when excessive current is drawn

Power strips essentially are connected in parallel with the building outlet and the devices. The technology device (e.g., computer) is then plugged in using a parallel connection into the power strip. For example, a computer is powered with 120 volts of AC. This AC goes into the power supply of the computer. The purpose of the power supply is to lower the voltage and to change the AC to a DC.

Most computers and technology devices contain a regulated power supply, which produces a more precise and constant output voltage. Regulated power supplies are fairly sophisticated devices, but the basic purpose is to reduce the 120 alternating voltage and change it to a constant DC. Figure 2.6 illustrates a simplification of a power supply circuit.

In a power supply, AC is generally converted into DC by the use of diodes or rectifiers. A selenium rectifier, for example, is commonly used for high-current rectification. The rectifier allows the current to flow in only one direction, which changes the AC to a DC. When diodes are used in a power supply, four silicon diodes are generally used to create a full-wave bridge rectifier which produces more effective rectification.

As illustrated in figure 2.6, the first component of a computer power supply is the electrical plug that has three-wire prongs connected to 120-volt AC from the power strip. One wire is the power line (hot line) and is generally colored black. The second wire is the neutral common ground and is colored white. The third wire is the safety ground and is colored green. This safety wire in generally screwed onto the frame of the power supply or computer.

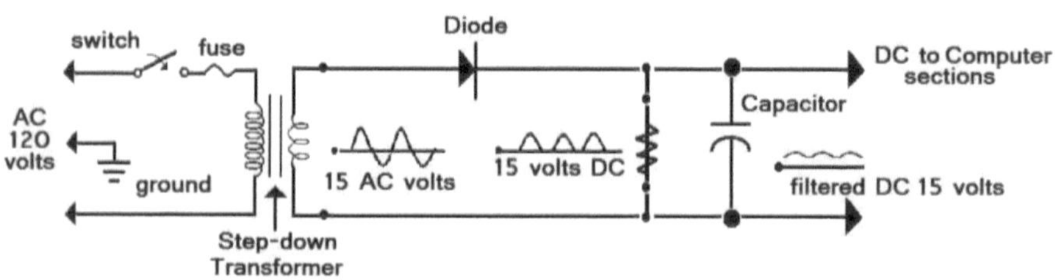

Figure 2.6. Simplification of an AC to DC power supply.

The safety ground is only necessary in the event of ground fault. This could occur if the power (hot) wire touches the frame of the power supply or computer. If this should happen, the electricity would flow to the area of least resistance and into the computer frame and ultimately to earth ground.

If the safety ground wire is not used, or is not properly connected to the frame, the electricity may flow through the person when the computer is touched. The person would probably incur a shock that could result in ventricular fibrillation or death. Therefore, never remove this third wire on the plug of the cord or the safety wire connected on the frame or power supply of the computer.

The next stage of power supply is the switch and fuse (see figure 2.6). The switch is used to control the AC supply for the power supply, which turns the computer on or off. The switch is often labeled as *I* or *O*. The *I* means the power is on and the *O* means power is off. Most switches used in computers and laptops are the push-button type, although toggle switches are sometimes used in larger computer applications.

All power supplies have a fuse that protects the computer from power overloads and surges. The fuse may be replaceable or soldered into the circuit. Fuses are rated in amperes. A typical computer fuse may range from 1 amp to 5 amps. Never replace a fuse with a higher rated fuse; doing so may destroy the computer. Also, some electronic devices use a circuit breaker instead of a fuse.

Once the AC passes through the switch and fuse, the next stage in the power supply is the *transformer* (see figure 2.6). The purpose of the transformer is to step-down the 120 alternating voltage entering the primary side of transformer to a lower voltage at the secondary side. This is accomplished by the reducing the number or size of the secondary windings of the transformer.

The voltages at the secondary side of the transformer typically range from 3 to 12 volts. The different voltages are used to supply different voltages to the circuits of the computer. For example, 12 volts could be used to power the disc drive motor and the lesser voltages could supply the external lights, central processing unit, and memory unit on the motherboard.

Once the voltage is reduced to these lower voltages, a rectifier must be used to convert the AC to DC. In figure 2.6, a diode is included in the circuit and converts the AC to a DC. However, at this point, the DC is a choppy voltage. These peaks and valleys of the DC are known as *ripple*.

This choppy DC needs to be filtered to create a smoother and more constant voltage. This is accomplished through the use of capacitors and other components. The ideal DC is stable and constant, and independent of voltage variations. The precision circuits in computers and other technology devices require a high-quality, regulated power supply to ensure uninterruptable and stable current.

For example, the *capacitor* in figure 2.6 shows a simplification of this regulating and filtering process. It changes the pulsating DC to a constant voltage by charging and discharging the capacitor to its original value. This quick charging and discharging creates a filtering process to allow the current to be a more regulated and constant DC.

More sophisticated regulated power supplies use a number of different components such as inductors and Zener diodes to act as voltage regulators to produce a constant, stable voltage. Power supplies also contain other components to provide voltage surge and heat protection. For example, a thermistor is type of resistor that varies in resistance depending on the temperature. It protects the circuit from drawing too much amperage because of excessive heat and causing the device to operate poorly or be damaged.

Another essential part of technology devices is the audio component. Audio receivers provide essential sound needed for instruction. A simplified description of a radio receiver is that it is an electronic device that picks up electromagnetic signals from the air and amplifies them to extract intelligence and produce audio sound. A typical audio wave travels at a speed of 300 million meters per second. The lower the frequency of an audio signal, the longer the wave. The higher a frequency of an audio signal, the shorter the wave.

A typical audio wave has a frequency between 20 Hz and 20,000 Hz (20 kHz). Sounds above 20 kHz cannot be heard by most people. Waves above 20 kHz are called *radio frequency* (RF) waves. Many audio receivers use amplitude modulation (AM). In AM transmission, a low-frequency audio wave is mixed with a high-frequency continuous wave. This produces an amplitude modulated radio wave that is transmitted and later received by a radio receiver.

Frequency modulation (FM) a technique of transmission that is more advanced than amplitude modulated transmission. The distance of the FM wave is much less than AM transmission, but the quality of signal is much higher. FM begins with an RF carrier wave and an audio frequency wave called the *modulating signal.* When the RF carrier wave is modulated with the audio signal, the frequency of the RF carrier varies with amplitude of the modulating signal.

Both AM and FM are considered *analog signal* applications. Analog signals are nonquantized variations that change continuously and vary in amplitude. Besides AM and FM signal transmission, many audio and video signals are transmitted digitally. Digital signals are produced by numerical digits and create even higher quality signals than FM transmission. Digital transmission and applications are explained in later chapters.

There are several types of computer monitors and smart televisions used in educational technology. These high-density televisions include liquid crystal display (LCD), digital light processing, LED, plasma, and ultra-high-definition television. These computer monitors and smart televisions have revolutionized education instruction. Unlike the older cathode ray tube (CRT), the produce clear images and brighter pictures, and enable larger screen sizes. They also are significantly thinner and lighter than the older CRT or projection televisions.

For example, LCD monitors and televisions operate by a series of capital fluorescent lamps at the base of the television screen. Millions of separate LCD shutters are composed on a grid formation that controls light emission. These are composed of tiny transistors and capacitors sometimes called *active matrix technology*. The light that passes through these shutters creates a color tone displayed in subpixels, which produces the image.

Plasma monitors and televisions work on a principle of a combination of electrically charged ionized gasses of tiny cells protected by a dialectic material. Gas flows through these cells and ultraviolet photons that are released create a visible light and image. The combinations of these colors produce a high-quality, bright-contrast picture.

Many types of transmissions are available for data communications in technology devices. Data can be transmitted through telephone lines, coaxial cable, fiber optic cable, microwave, and satellite. There are many traditional coaxial cable transmissions and wireless transmissions that remain popular. The pulses of light that form the electromagnetic carrier wave are the basis of fiber optic communication.

Fiber-optic communications are useful for long-distance applications as compared with traditional communication wiring systems. Fiber-optic communication is accomplished with the LED transmitter, which has the ability to produce excellent data transmission. When data are received, an optical receiver converts the light signal to an electrical form by using a photo diode and other optical detectors.

While fiber-optic cable was initially more expensive and time consuming to install, the technology now has become common. Specialized cable, which often includes armored coatings, prevents intrusion and mechanical or toxic damage. Vertical cavity surface–emitting lasers can also be used to provide significantly higher communications properties and power than LEDs.

UNDERSTANDING TROUBLESHOOTING METHODS

Every technology educator should understand some basic troubleshooting and maintenance of technology devices. The principles of troubleshooting begin with having a good sense of problem-solving techniques and hands-on skills. When attempting to troubleshoot a device, begin with three phases: situational analysis, problem solving, and decision making.

Always proceed in a logical manner; otherwise mistakes, accidents, and wasted time may occur. For example, you may reset a circuit breaker just to experience the breaker tripping again because you failed to unplug a shorted device. Also, never replace a fuse with a higher amperage-rated fuse or damage could result to the device.

Begin by asking questions and making observations in the first phase, called *situational analysis*. Discuss the defect with any users; compare the problem with others from your past experiences. Note any symptoms or relevant changes that might have occurred. Use your senses and identify any unusual smells, sounds, or visual damage.

The second phase consists of *problem solving*. This is the stage in which you obtain necessary manufacturer's service manuals or product manuals, which typically have a step-by-step troubleshooting guide. Do not short change this process by attempting to solve the problem without first reading these materials. Typical problems may be poor connections, wrong input connections, improper power supply, or physical damage.

Once you have identified the cause of the problem, the last step is *decision making*. This step is defined as examining various solutions and selecting the best option. It is necessary to consider all the advantages and disadvantages for each alternative. For example, you may need to obtain a better video software, printer, keyboard, power strip, computer, monitor, or projector. All of these devices have varying degrees of cost and quality. Using these three phases of troubleshooting can provide a foundation for becoming an expert troubleshooter.

Some of the typical circuit faults as previously presented include excessive heat, moisture, contaminants, poor installation, and manufacturing defects, among other problems. The use of excessive heat applied to any electronic device can damage circuits and components. It can cause materials to expand, crack, blister, and prematurely break down. Likewise, moisture can cause circuits to draw more current and short circuit.

Moisture and other liquids can also cause expansion, warping, and abnormal current flow. Therefore, when troubleshooting technology devices, look for these obvious circuit fault contributors as well as any loose wires, poor connections, improper connections, and read the product manual to ensure correct installation and operation.

Besides troubleshooting, every educator should be responsible and maintain the technology equipment. Often devices break down and can be directly attributed to operator abuse. Periodic cleaning of technology devices can help prevent breakdowns and longevity. Dirty circuits create increased heat in a circuit and prematurely break down components.

Dusty, dirty circuit boards and power supplies can create arching and damage.

Periodically carefully cleaning the back of a computer using a vacuum cleaner can help remove dust and dirt. Likewise, keep all devices clean and free from food and liquids. For example, never allow food and liquid to compromise the keyboard. Also, use available commercially produced products to help keep your equipment clean and maintained.

Remember to use common safety and protective electronic devices. Use product safety and protective shields and never replace a polarized three-pronged plug with a nonpolarized two pronged plug. The polarized plug helps prevent you from becoming part of the electrical circuit. Severe shock and damage to the device, as well as the user, can occur.

SUMMARY

The building block of electricity is the structure of matter. All matter, such as air, water, and the earth, are made up of very small particles called *atoms*. The structure of an atom consists of an inner core called a *nucleus* that contains protons and neutrons. Electrons orbit around the nucleus and carry a negative charge. Protons have a positive charge and neutrons are neutral.

The definition of *electricity* is the flow of electrons in a circuit. Electricity consists of three fundamental unites called *voltage, amperage,* and *resistance.* Ohm's Law is the theory used to calculate the interrelationships between them.

All materials have properties of being a conductor, insulator, or semiconductor. Conductors are materials such as copper and silver. Good insulators are rubber and glass. Examples of semiconductors are silicon or germanium.

Common circuit combinations are called *series, parallel,* and *series-parallel circuits.* They are formed through the use of electronic components. Typical components include diodes, transistors, capacitors, inductors, and switches. For example, two diodes back-to-back form a transistor. A transistor is used for switching and amplifying and is generally a pnp or npn type.

The power supply contains a transformer that converts a high voltage to a lower voltage. Diodes can be used to rectify AC to DC. A typical power supply consists of several components such as fuses, diodes, capacitors, and inductors. Power supplies are used in most educational technology devices.

Educators should always practice safety when using technology devices. No matter how competent you feel you are, a troubleshooter must respect the power of electricity and practice proper safety considerations. Electricity can cause significant damage to the human body ranging from small burns to neurological damage and even death.

Physiological effects to the body can be created with as little as 200 mA of current directly applied to a person's heart. Always read the product manual when operating, maintaining, and troubleshooting technology devices. Lastly, use care and keep your technology equipment clean and well maintained.

CASE STUDY

You are a new technology educator and have just started working at an educational institution. Your supervisor has asked you to draw and explain a schematic diagram outlining the electrical current from an outlet to the circuits in a computer. Explain the typical voltages, rectifying process, and components. Describe several safety considerations that all technology educators should follow when using technology devices.

Also, list and describe several common faults with technology equipment and devices. Finally, outline some typical troubleshooting techniques for identifying electronic problems and maintaining and repairing electronic equipment and devices.

EXERCISES AND DISCUSSION QUESTIONS

1. Explain the structure of matter and definition of electricity.
2. Describe Ohm's Law and the purpose and differences between series, parallel, and series-parallel circuits.
3. List at least six different electronic components, their purpose, and symbols.
4. Describe the typical operation of an electronic power supply.

REFERENCES

Tomal, D. (2010). *Action research for educators*. Lanham, MD: Roman & Littlefield Education.

Tomal, D., & Agajanian, A. (2014). *Electronic troubleshooting*. New York: McGraw-Hill.

THREE

Computer Peripherals

OBJECTIVES

At the conclusion of the chapter, the reader will be able to:

1. Understand what peripheral devices are and why people use them (ISTE 1, 3, 6).
2. Describe the basic types of peripheral devices (ISTE 3, 6).
3. Explain how to connect and use peripheral devices (ISTE 3, 6).
4. Describe the basic types of connectors used by most computer systems and peripheral devices (ISTE 3, 6).
5. Explain what steps to take to troubleshoot general peripheral device connection problems (ISTE 3, 6).

OVERVIEW AND FUNCTION OF PERIPHERALS

What are peripherals? Why do we need them? How do we set them up? What do we do when they don't work? "Peripherals" or "computer peripherals" are devices that can be connected to a computer to provide additional functionality. Common examples of peripheral devices include printers, keyboards, scanners, and computer mice.

A computer is basically a machine that performs logical mathematical computations quickly. Modern peripheral devices allow people to interact with these powerful machines in intuitive, useful, and sometimes exciting ways. Developing an understanding of how peripheral devices generally work can help a person use computer systems more effectively and troubleshoot problems more efficiently.

Computer systems can be purchased in a variety of configurations. Most include a suite of standard peripherals that are essential for interacting with modern computer systems. A keyboard, mouse, and display device are usually among the standard set. Sometimes these peripherals

Figure 3.1. External and integrated peripherals of desktop and laptop computers. (Courtesy Dell Inc.)

are separate external components as seen in a typical "desktop" computer system. These components can also be integrated into the computer system itself as seen in a typical "laptop" computer system (figure 3.1). Other peripherals can be added to provide more functionality to an existing system.

Technically speaking, all peripherals work by sending data into the system and receiving data out of the system—they are all "input-output" devices—but peripherals are often categorized by the primary function they perform:

- Input
- Output
- Storage
- Communication

Input devices are a category of peripherals that enable a computer to receive input from the physical environment. These include keyboards, mice, microphones, webcams, document scanners, and graphic tablets. Specialized input peripherals like magnetic card readers, fingerprint scanners, and motion detectors allow a computer system to receive input from other specialized physical sources. Choosing the right type of input device can make interactions with a computer much easier.

Output devices are a category of peripherals that enable a computer to send information back to the physical environment. Output devices use information from computers to generate sounds we can hear, images we can see, printed things we can hold, and so on. Devices in this category include speakers, liquid crystal display (LCD) monitors, laser printers, and video projectors. Specialized output peripherals like 3D printers and robotic arms allow a computer system to send output to the physical world in interesting specialized ways.

Storage devices are a category of peripherals that allow a computer to store data on a variety of media. All computer systems come with built-in storage of some form, but eventually the capacity of the built-in storage will be reached. Peripheral storage devices enable the expansion of storage capacity. Examples of storage devices include magnetic hard drives, optical DVD writers, and solid-state flash drives.

Communication devices are a category of peripherals that enable a computer to communicate with other computer-based systems. Many communication capabilities are usually included as part of a base computer system. For example, most modern computers are shipped with Ethernet ports or wireless antennas. But communication device peripherals can expand communication options. Examples include digital subscriber line modems, cable modems, network interfaces devices, and musical instrument digital interface devices.

Some devices span these categories by performing multiple functions. "All-in-one" devices that print and scan are common. Force-feedback devices that accept input (e.g., through a steering wheel) and provide feedback (through vibrations and steering wheel resistance) are used in many gaming and virtual world simulation applications. Some newer laptop touchpads accept standard finger movement input and also provide haptic feedback back to the user.

Choosing the right type of peripheral can often lead to more efficient and effective computer use. For example, an art student can draw diagrams far more precisely by using a graphics tablet than by using a mouse. Text from a printed page can be converted into electronic text much more quickly with a scanner and optical character recognition software than through manual typing on a keyboard. A teacher showing a presentation to a large group of students will find that using a high-powered video projector is appropriate, while a medical student analyzing x-rays will be better served using a high-resolution desktop LCD monitor.

CONNECTING AND USING

To use a new peripheral device with a computer, it is important to understand that all peripherals need the appropriate connection hardware and appropriate supporting software. Why is this the case? A typical peripheral device like a keyboard or mouse requires a physical connection, like a cable with electrical wires, to carry information to and from a computer. Without the physical connection provided by the cable, there would be no way for the peripheral to send signals to the computer.

Special supporting software, often called a *device driver*, is also needed by a computer to serve as a kind of translator between the computer and

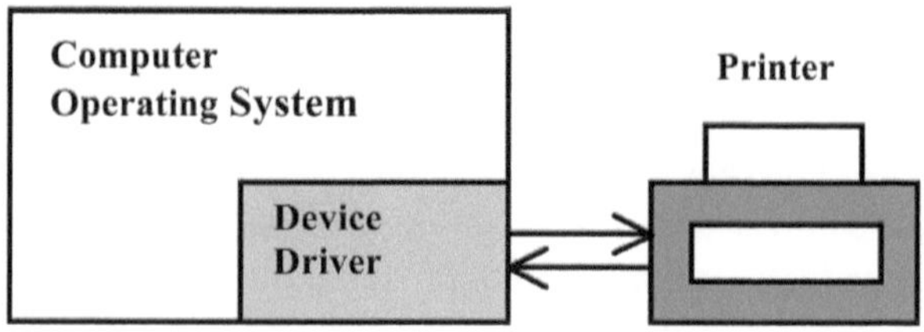

Figure 3.2. Device drivers and communication with peripherals.

the peripheral. Device drivers are programs that run on a computer; they allow the computer to understand the meaning of signals received from the peripheral device. They also allow a computer to send appropriate command signals to the device (figure 3.2).

For example, printers made by Hewlett-Packard (HP) may require one set of signals to tell them to print in blue ink, while printers made by Epson may require different signals to tell them to print in blue ink. The HP driver enables a computer to send the right set of signals to the HP printer, and the Epson driver enables a computer to send the right set of signals to the Epson printer. Each peripheral device is typically shipped with device drivers for various computer systems.

The main ideas behind hardware and software for making connections to peripherals are simple. However, it is helpful to understand some of the details related to choosing the right connection hardware, and the details for making sure the software is working correctly. Installing new peripherals and troubleshooting peripherals that are not working properly require this more detailed level of understanding.

Connection Hardware

The most common type of physical connector for peripheral devices currently is a universal serial bus (USB) connector. USB was first introduced as a standard in 1996. Its purpose was to help simplify physical connections between computers and peripherals. Most keyboards, mice, printers, and hard drives can be connected to modern computer systems with a standard USB cable and plug.

Prior to the introduction of USB, each device usually had a different specialized connector that also required the target computer system to have all the necessary specialized ports. As a result, many computer systems needed to be preequipped with a large number of specialized ports for printers, keyboards, mice, and any other peripheral devices that might be connected to the computer system. Some peripherals even came with expansion cards with specialized ports that had to be manually installed by opening a computer's case.

With USB, the situation is simplified. A computer can be equipped with one type of port, and all manner of devices can be physically connected through that one type of USB port. Furthermore, the USB standard includes many other useful features, including the ability to send device power through the USB cable. A single USB port can be expanded to multiple ports through the use of USB hubs and through "daisy-chaining" (connecting several devices sequentially in a chain). These additional features are useful when space limits the number of built-in ports in smaller computer systems like laptops.

Within the USB connector family, there are also subcategories of connectors like USB Type A, USB Type B, and micro-USB. Some of these are variations of the connector to accommodate the different physical sizes of devices. For example, small devices like smartphones are more likely to use the smaller micro-USB port. There are many adapters that allow various types of USB connectors and cables to work with each other. Figure 3.3 shows examples of various USB connectors.

The USB connector family also includes connectors that conform to different versions of the USB standard. They may look the similar on the outside, but the version will affect the rate of data transfer the connector can support. The standard introduced in 1996 is now called USB 1.0. Newer USB 2.0 and USB 3.0 devices and cables are far more common today, and permit much faster data transmission speeds.

For comparison, a USB 1.0 device and cable could theoretically transfer data at a rate of 12 megabits per second (Mbit/s), which works out to 12,000,000 bits of information per second. A USB 3.0 device can

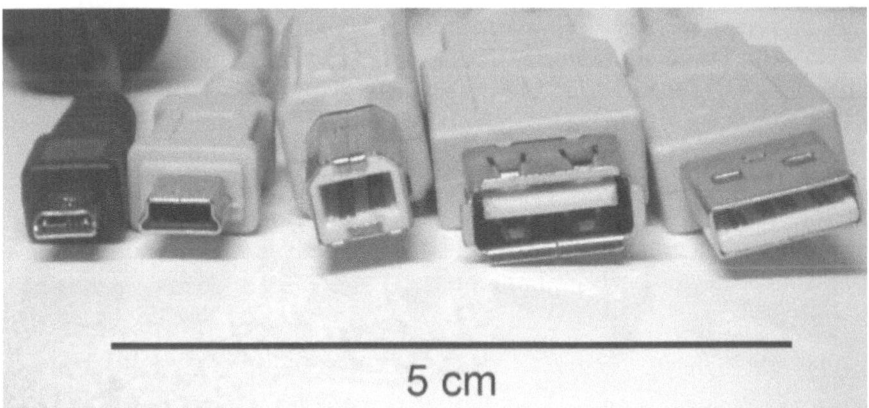

Figure 3.3. Examples of various types of USB connectors.

theoretically transfer data at a rate of 5 gigabits per second (Gbit/s), which works out to 5,000,000,000 bits of information per second, which is over four hundred times faster than USB 1.0 (Mearian, 2011). The big lesson to take from this is that the higher the USB version, the faster the potential rate of data transfer.

There are other competing physical connection standards including FireWire and Thunderbolt. Typically, computers running Windows will have only USB ports, while computers from the Apple Macintosh family usually have a combination of USB, Thunderbolt, and FireWire ports. These standards have performance differences that make them better for certain applications like video-editing work on external hard drives. For example, the Thunderbolt 3 standard claims to have a maximum data transfer rate of 40 Gbit/s, which is fast enough to even work as a high-definition video monitor connector (Hruska, 2014).

Another type of physical connection is a wireless connection. In a wireless communication situation, there is still a physical connection. However, information is not sent through wires of a cable. Instead, information is sent through electromagnetic signals traveling through the air and walls from an antenna in the computer to an antenna in the peripheral device. Two popular wireless connection technologies for peripherals are Bluetooth and Wi-Fi. Bluetooth is usually used to connect a device directly to a computer, while Wi-Fi is usually used to connect a device to an existing wireless computer network.

Some of the main advantages of a wireless connection include greater convenience and the reduction of workspace clutter caused by numerous cables and cords. Users do not have to repeatedly plug and unplug a device cable, or search for just the right kind of adapter. Some of the main disadvantages of a wireless connection include slower communication speeds, greater security concerns, and lower communication reliability. Unlike wired signals, which travel along one designated path, wireless signals can go in all directions and are potentially vulnerable to someone "listening in"—even with modern security protocols.

To summarize, when attaching a new peripheral device, at the very least an appropriate physical connection is needed. A connector from the USB family, a connector from another family like Thunderbolt, or a completely wireless connection can be chosen. It all depends on the peripheral's built-in connector ports and antennas and the computer system's built-in connector ports and antennas.

Supporting Software

As mentioned earlier, even after devices are physically connected (whether by USB, Thunderbolt, or some other means), a computer system needs to have the appropriate supporting software installed. The supporting software is typically called a *device driver*. Device drivers are essential for enabling a computer to actually work with a peripheral device.

Each peripheral device manufacturer has its own way of making the driver software available. Some provide an installation DVD. Others require users to download the drivers from the company website. Still others have the drivers stored on the device itself; the drivers are installed when the device is first plugged into a computer. Many external storage devices and wireless clicker devices do this. Computer companies also ship their operating systems (like Microsoft Windows and MacOS X) preinstalled with a large set of drivers for various popular brands of printers and other common peripheral devices like keyboards and mice.

Software device drivers, like other programs that run on a computer, are not perfect and are susceptible to problems. Sometimes they crash and stop working. Other times, the driver's preference files can become damaged, rendering the software ineffective. Some software device drivers are poorly written and just do not work well with various computer systems. It is also not uncommon for drivers to stop working when an operating system is updated.

Device drivers are technically examples of system software. They behave like translators between a computer and a peripheral. People do not interact directly with device drivers. Instead, a secondary type of software called *application software* is needed to interact with a computer and a peripheral device (figure 3.4). Microsoft Word, Firefox, and Photoshop are examples of application software.

Many printers are shipped with only device drivers. The expectation is that most computer systems will already have application software like word processors installed on them, and so printer manufacturers can provide just the device drivers. On the other hand, many scanners are shipped with both device drivers and some application software. Canon usually includes a version of MP Navigator and Epson provides a version of Epson Scan. Even when application software is provided, it is still

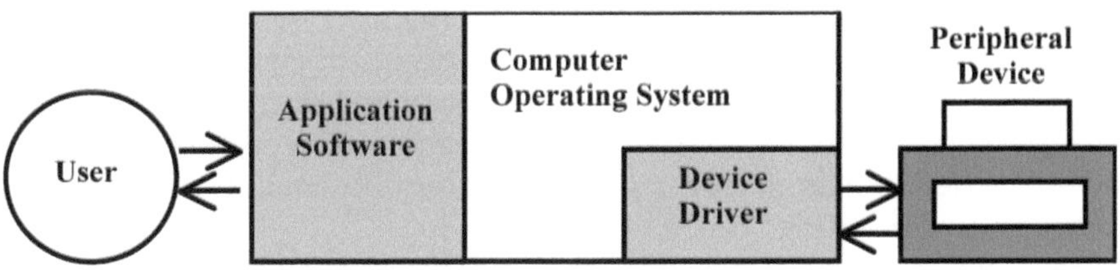

Figure 3.4. Application software and device drivers.

possible to use another application like Photoshop, to interact with a new scanner through the scanner's device drivers.

To summarize, for a new peripheral device to work with a computer system, at the very least device drivers (system software) must be installed. Sometimes the device drivers are preinstalled in the operating system (for common peripherals like mice, keyboards, and many printers) and at other times, they must be installed from the provided installer disk or online download. Existing application software, or application software provided by the peripheral manufacturer, can be then be used to interact with the new peripheral.

TROUBLESHOOTING AND MAINTENANCE

For any computer system and peripheral device combination, the general approach for troubleshooting is as follows:

1. Check the physical connection.
2. Check the supporting software.

To begin, with any peripheral device connected to a computer system, (1) the physical connection needs to be secure. A FireWire, USB, or Ethernet plug that has not been fully pushed in will cause problems. Removing and reinserting a loose connector will fix many issues. Sometimes in public lab settings, cords and connectors are exposed to a lot of wear and tear. Connectors should therefore be inspected for possible damage. Wires often fray at the joint where a flexible wire meets a rigid connector. Connectors exhibiting damage should be replaced.

If a peripheral's connection is made over a wireless network, the network settings on the device should be checked. The device should be connected to the same wireless network the computer is using. In some facilities, there may be multiple networks available at a given spot (maybe an administrators' network and a public network), and it is usually necessary for both the peripheral device and the computer to be on the same network.

If the physical connection appears to be fine and there are still problems, the next step is to (2) check the supporting software for the peripheral device. Investigating the settings of a peripheral's control panel or the settings of a peripheral's diagnostic software should occur first. Depending on the device manufacturer, one or both may be available. Confirming device software settings can lead to a quick fix.

For example, an external speaker may not be working because the mute box has been checked—figure 3.5 shows a MacOS X sound control panel

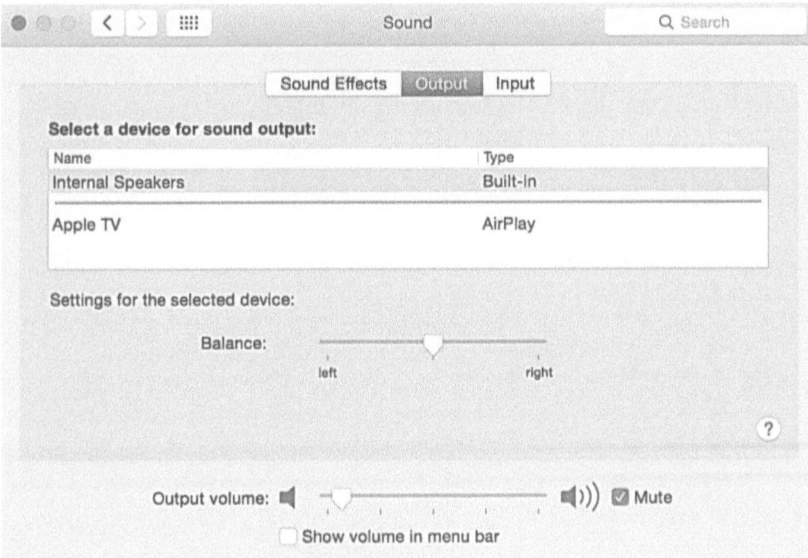

Figure 3.5. Macintosh sound control panel.

with the mute box checked. A microphone may not be accepting input because it has not been selected among the many input options in the sound control panel. Sometimes, a nonresponsive printer can be fixed by simply making sure it is chosen as the target printer in the printer settings control panel.

If the settings appear to be correct and the device is still not fully functional, there may be a problem with the device driver software. One simple way to fix a software driver issue is to restart the computer and restart the peripheral device. Restarting fixes many problems, including device drivers that may have crashed.

If that does not work, for some operating systems, diagnostic software can be used to check device driver functionality. For example, on a computer system running the Windows 7 operating system, the Device Manager control panel can be opened from the list of all control panel items. As shown in figure 3.6, the Device Manager lists all the devices connected to the computer. Right-clicking on a device reveals options for updating drivers or even uninstalling device software. Devices experiencing problems often have an error icon next to the device name.

If this approach is not successful, completely reinstalling the driver and other related software should be tried next. This can be done using the device's installation DVD or by downloading and running the necessary installers from the device manufacturer's website. After the reinstallation

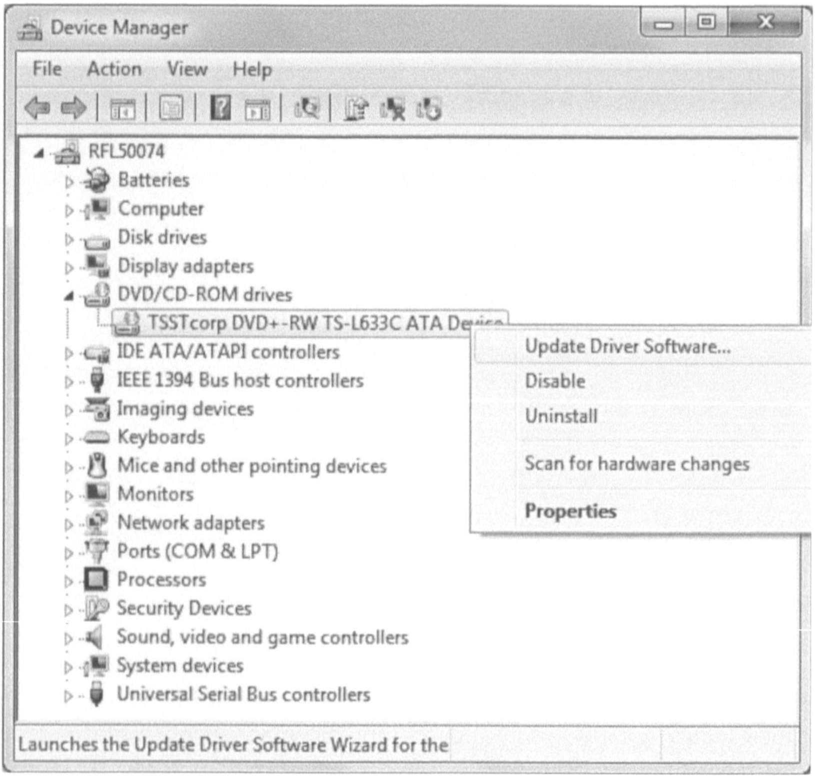

Figure 3.6. Windows Device Manager and drivers.

of the drivers, both the computer and device should be restarted. A clean version of the drivers and the restart is highly likely to fix most problems.

These steps are generally applicable to most peripheral devices. The details for each step can vary slightly depending on the peripheral device type, peripheral device brand, the connectors used, and the operating system of a computer. Tips for understanding, maintaining, and troubleshooting a few common peripheral devices will be provided in the next section of this chapter.

Mice and Keyboards

Most external mice and external keyboards use a USB connector. Both require some electrical power, which the USB connector provides from the computer. For example, an optical mouse requires power for the small lights and sensor circuitry. When connected and working properly, a computer provides a mouse and keyboard with electrical power, and the mouse and keyboard send input information from the user to the computer.

Mice and keyboards are durable peripherals that don't require a lot of maintenance. However, some common-sense practices help these devices remain functional. For example, food, water, dirt, and dust should generally be kept away. Cords connecting mice and keyboards should not be pinched or stretched, and the devices themselves should not be dropped. Regular cleaning and vacuuming can help keep keys and buttons from sticking.

When a mouse or keyboard is not working properly, check the physical connections to see whether electrical power is running properly to the device. This can be done by looking to see whether the usual status lights are on. For example, optical mice have a little light on the bottom that should remain on. If the light is not on, try plugging the mouse into another USB port or into a USB port on another computer. If the light turns on in these alternate configurations, there is a chance that the first USB port itself is damaged and may need to be replaced. Damage that results in insufficient power being sent to devices is not uncommon.

For simple mice and keyboards, software problems are rare. However, for mice and keyboards with extra programmable buttons, there is a chance the software settings may not be correct. In addition to restarting the computer, read through the installation guide that came with the keyboard to adjust device software settings properly.

Printers

Printers are probably the most common type of peripheral that can be added to a computer system. The two main types of consumer-level printers are laser printers and inkjet printers. Laser printers use a laser to "draw" images on a rolling, light-sensitive drum. The drum picks up toner and transfers that onto paper. Inkjet printers work by spraying tiny dots of ink directly onto paper.

Each type of printer has its strengths and weaknesses. Laser printers tend to be more expensive to purchase, but then cost less to print per page. They tend to excel with black-and-white documents and can print very fast. Inkjet printers are less expensive initially, but regularly replenishing ink can be costly. Inkjet printers produce good black-and-white documents as well as highly detailed color documents. They are typically slower than laser printers for black and white, but usually produce more vibrant color documents than a comparable color laser printer.

Because of these traits, laser printers are often used as "shared printers" for high volume black and white document printing, while inkjet printers are often used for less frequent color printing by individuals. Even with the differences in actual printing technology, the technologies used by printers for communicating with other computing devices tend to be the same. Most printers are equipped with USB ports or Ethernet ports. Some have built-in wireless network antennas. The data transmission speed requirements of printers are not very high, and so USB 2.0 connectors and wireless connections are typically more than sufficient.

A USB connection is usually used when a printer is set up to communicate directly with just one computer at a time. Printers connected directly to a computer through a USB cable generally communicate and print reliably. On occasion, printing may not occur properly when users have been sending print requests to multiple printers. This can be solved by manually reselecting the desired target USB printer through a printers control panel. Figure 3.7 shows the Printers and Scanners control panel for MacOS X. People using laptops in various settings may sometimes encounter this type of problem.

The Ethernet port is usually used when a printer is set up to be a shared printer that receives print requests from multiple computers on an existing computer network. Wireless network antennas allow a shared printer to connect to a computer network without the use of more cables. Wired and wireless network connections provide sufficiently fast data connection speeds for most printers.

Printers connected to a network generally work reliably as well. Unexpected outages to network services or power can lead to network printing

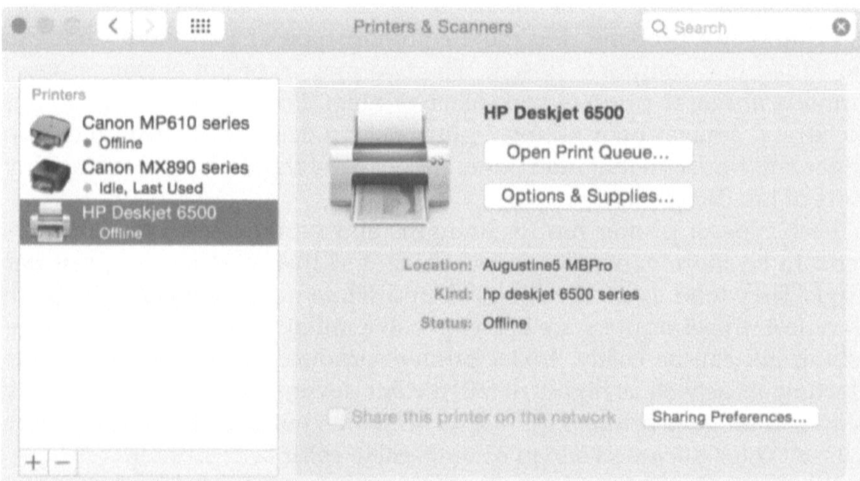

Figure 3.7. MacOS X Printers and Scanners control panel.

Figure 3.8. Network printer and printer control panel. (Courtesy Dell Inc.)

problems. Depending on how the printer and network were originally configured, an interruption can lead to various settings (like the network address of the printer) being changed inadvertently.

If printing problems do occur, the settings on the printer itself should be checked. First, the wired or wireless network connection should be confirmed through the use of the printer's built-in diagnostic tools. These are accessible through the printer's control panel (usually located on the front of the printer, as in figure 3.8). The printer's network name should also be verified because an unexpected power outage can cause a printer's settings to reset to a default name.

If printer settings appear to be correct, then the software settings on the computer should be checked. The printer control panel should be examined to make sure the target printer has been selected. If it appears to be selected but printing does not work, sometimes deleting the printer from the list of choices and adding it again will help fix the problem. Other times, installing the latest printer driver from the printer manufacturer's website will help.

Printers can also function improperly when ink and paper supplies are insufficient. Paper is more likely to jam when there are only a couple of sheets remaining, so keeping the paper tray well stocked will prevent jamming. When ink or toner supplies get low, the quality of printed pages can be negatively affected with images and text looking faded or lighter than usual.

A dusty environment can also have a negative influence on a printer. With a laser printer, dirty components can lead to streaking on printed pages. Ink jet printer nozzles can get clogged, leading to inferior output. Keeping the printer environment relatively clean will help, as will the occasional running of a print head "cleaning" cycle on ink jet printer for example.

Scanners

Scanners are another common type of peripheral that can be added to a computer system. Most scanners use USB ports, but some "network scanners" offer Ethernet and wireless options as well. Like other peripheral devices, scanners require appropriate software drivers to work with computers. Most scanners available currently use USB 2.0 connectors, with a few now offering USB 3.0. When scanning in high resolution, the resulting image files can be very large, so scanners are a category of devices that would benefit from faster USB 3.0 speeds.

Scanners do not require a lot of maintenance, but they do require careful handling. Heavy objects like books should not be left on top of flatbed scanners. Internal components can become compressed and the glass scanner bed can become loose over time. The scanner glass should be cleaned regularly to reduce dust and smudges that can show up on scanned document images. Scanners with paper-feed mechanisms should be dusted and vacuumed regularly to reduce the accumulation of dust on rolling components that handle the paper. Dirty rollers can lead to paper jams.

Troubleshooting scanner problems follows the same basic "connection hardware" and "supporting software" checking. The wired or wireless connection should be verified first, and then software settings on the computer should be checked. This can be done using a scanner control panel, like the MacOS X example in figure 3.7. Running an application program from the scanner manufacturer can also help with troubleshooting. Some scanner programs offer specific error messages like "scanner not connected" or "scanner drivers not installed."

When working in a situation with multiple scanners and scanner models, there are some additional things to consider. If the hardware appears to be correctly connected and the software drivers appear to be functional, the specific application program choice should be checked. Some scanner manufacturers have specific versions of their scanning application that work with specific scanner models.

For example, Canon's MP Navigator EX 4.0 program will work with many Canon scanners, but not with Canon's MX892 all-in-one device. To use the scanning features of the MX892 device, Canon's MP Navigator EX 5.1 program needs to be used. The 5.1 version of MP Navigator does not work with many of the devices compatible with 4.0 version of MP Navigator.

Check the installation DVD or the manufacturer's website to find the right version of application software for your device. Compatibility between a specific scanner model and specific application software version should be verified. It should not be assumed that scanning software from a manufacturer will work with all of its scanning device models.

External Hard Drives

External hard drives come in many shapes and sizes. Some can draw power from a computer's USB port, while others require a separate power supply. Some offer connections through both USB and FireWire, and others require one specific type of connection technology. For most modern external hard drives connected to modern computer systems, working with files should be just as fast as working with files on an internal hard drive.

Typically, hard drives are categorized by their physical size and disk rotational speed. Portable drives are usually 2.5 inches wide while stationary hard drives are usually 3.5 inches wide. Most hard drives spin at 5,400 or 7,200 rotations per second, although they can range from 4,200 to 15,000 rotations per second. The faster the hard drive spins, the faster data can be accessed from the hard drive. Faster hard drives tend to be more expensive and use more power.

Even though some external drives are labeled "portable," hard drives in general are delicate devices that should be handled carefully. Hard drives contain stacks of thin magnetic disks spinning at speeds of up to 15,000 rotations per minute, with read-write heads floating a few nanometers over the spinning disks (Boettcher, Li, de Callafon, & Talke, 2011). While safety mechanisms are built into many modern hard drives, jostling or knocking over a spinning drive can lead to drive damage and data loss. Excessive heat can reduce hard drive life as well, so external drives should be placed in a clean and appropriately ventilated location.

Hard drives do not require a lot of external physical maintenance—just keep them relatively dust free and cool, and don't drop them. However, they do benefit from occasional checking and maintenance through the use of disk utility software. Disk utilities included with Windows and MacOS X operating systems provide basic disk verification and repair services.

For example, with the Windows 7 operating system, the Properties window of a hard drive can be opened by right clicking on a hard disk icon and selecting "Properties." Clicking on the "Tools" tab will then reveal a set of disk maintenance functions (figure 3.9). Clicking on the "Check now" button opens a dialog window that offers options for automatically fixing file system errors and for attempting to recover data on bad sectors of the hard disk (see figure 3.9).

With the MacOS X operating system, the Disk Utility program can be used for basic disk verification and repair services. Disk Utility can be found in the Utilities folder inside the main Applications folder. As shown in figure 3.10, a user can select a disk in Disk Utility and then click on either the "Verify Disk" or "Repair Disk" buttons.

When hard drive problems do occur, the connection hardware should be checked first. For example, if an external hard drive appears to be operating at a much lower speed than anticipated, one possible culprit is the cable itself. As mentioned earlier in this chapter, the USB family has a number of versions available, with USB version 3.0 being the fastest. However, Type A connectors for USB 1.0, USB 2.0, and USB 3.0, are the same shape and fit into each other's ports. Connecting a USB 3.0 hard drive with a USB 2.0 cable will result in severely diminished performance.

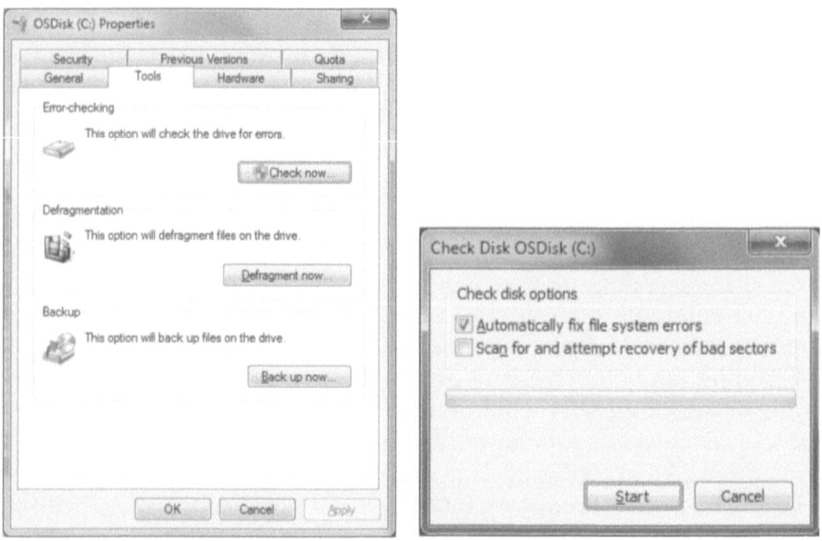

Figure 3.9. Example of disk properties for Windows 7.

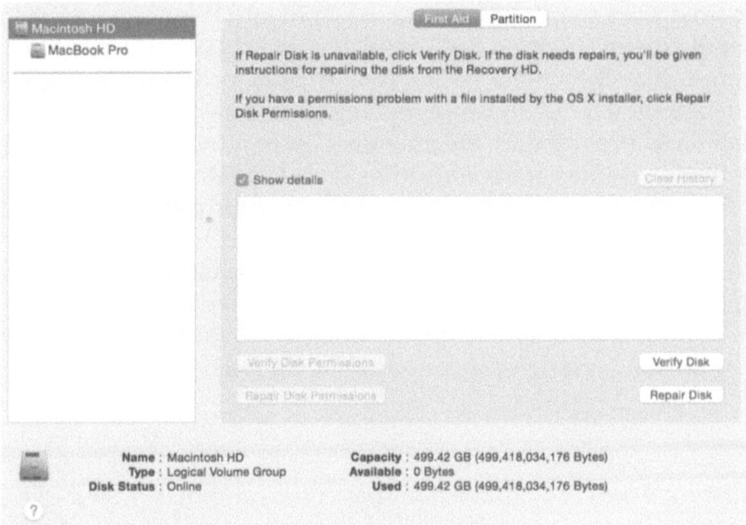

Figure 3.10. Example of disk utility for MacOS X.

Distinguishing marks, like colors on the plugs, can help users figure out what type of cable is being used. However, a USB 2.0 cable can still be inserted into the port of a USB 3.0 hard drive without any problems. In this situation, the data transmission speed would be at most 35 Mbit/s because that is the limit of USB 2.0 cables. By comparison, if a USB 3.0 cable is used with a USB 3.0 hard drive, the data transmission speed can be as high as 5,000 Mbit/s. With hard drives—and also with other storage devices like solid state drives—using the right matching cable is essential for enabling the fastest data transmission speeds.

Hard drives using FireWire connection technology will not have this particular problem. FireWire 400 connectors are a different size and shape compared with FireWire 800 connectors. The wrong type of FireWire cable cannot be used with FireWire drives because they are physically incompatible.

When the physical connections appear to be correct and the hard drive still does not function properly, there may be issues with the hard drive itself. Hard drive directories can become corrupted and the magnetic media of the disks can start to degrade. The range of possible problems is broad, and so the best approach is to use a comprehensive disk utility application.

As mentioned earlier, Windows and MacOS X have basic built-in disk utilities. For Windows 7, the Properties window and the Disk Management tool may be used together. For MacOS X the Disk Utility application can be used. Disk management features built into Windows and MacOS X can handle many common disk problems. Third-party disk utilities from companies like Symantec, Avanquest, ALSoft, and Prosoft Engineering provide additional maintenance and repair features that are more powerful than those provided by the operating system tools.

If software utilities are unable to repair a hard drive, the drive may require reformatting or repartitioning. These can be performed using Disk Management in Windows or Disk Utility in MacOS X. If any data needs to be recovered, special data recovery services should be employed before reformatting. If a hard drive starts to make frequent loud clicking noises, or the spinning disk sound grows from a soft hum to a loud whine, chances are the hard drive will need to be replaced completely.

Displays

Display devices are an essential part of a computer system. Displays used for computers are often called *computer monitors* or just *monitors*. They provide the primary visual feedback to users. Computer monitors are available in a variety of shapes, sizes, and resolutions, and they use a variety of connector types. Most displays require the user to look directly at the display screen, but some displays project an image onto an external screen or a wall. Some computers support and can display images on multiple monitors simultaneously.

Display Characteristics

Cathode ray tube (CRT) monitors were once the most popular type of display. Large boxy televisions used CRT technology. However, computer monitors using LCD and plasma display panel (PDP) technologies are far more popular currently. LCD and PDP monitors are flat and thin, instead of big and boxy. They are lighter and usually use significantly less power than CRT monitors. Many newer LCD displays use light-emitting diodes (LEDs) to provide the backlight for the LCD monitor. This type of LCD monitor is also referred to as an *LED monitor,* and uses less power than older LCD displays.

Projection display devices for computers are usually called *video projectors*. Many projectors use LCD technology as a part of the projection system, and so they are also sometimes called *LCD projectors*. Other competing projection technologies include digital light processing (DLP) and liquid crystal on silicon (LCoS). LCD projectors are popular because, for the same cost, they provide better contrast and brightness than DLP and LCoS.

The size of monitors is obviously an important physical dimension. Size is often given as the diagonal measure of the display screen. For example, a 15-inch monitor measures 15 inches from one corner of the screen to the other diagonal corner. Another equally important physical dimension of displays is the screen resolution. Resolution is usually denoted by a pair of numbers like 1024 × 768, which means for example that a screen has 1024 pixels (or "dots of light") horizontally and 768 pixels vertically.

Images on a 15-inch monitor with a resolution of 2048 × 1080 will be sharper than images on a 15-inch monitor with a resolution of 1024 × 768. This is because there are more pixels in the same given area. Therefore, a monitor with the higher resolution will be able to display images with much finer detail.

Greater visual detail is attractive to view, but also leads to higher data requirements for the monitor and computer. Many computers have dedicated graphics processing units that generate high-resolution display information. They also need to use high-speed digital connectors to send graphics information rapidly to high-resolution monitors.

A variety of physical connectors are available for use with monitors. Depending on the age of a monitor, it may have some combination of video graphics array (VGA), digital video interface (DVI), or high-definition multimedia interface (HDMI) ports available. Newer monitors tend to use digital connection technologies like DVI and HDMI, while older monitors tend to use analog connection technologies like VGA. As expected, higher resolution monitors require the newer high-speed digital connection technologies.

Display Troubleshooting

Regardless of what type of monitor is being used, when display problems occur, in most cases the problem is with the physical connection from the computer to the monitor. Making sure the connector is plugged into the correct port on both the computer and monitor is often the best first step to troubleshooting. With monitors that have multiple ports, users need to make sure the monitor is using information from the correct video source. Many devices either have a dedicated source button or the source can be selected from an onscreen menu.

Video projectors often have additional features that can lead to problems. For example, many projectors have both "input" and "output" video ports that look physically identical. These are provided so a user can project an image on a screen and at the same time send that video signal to computer monitor. In this type of situation, checking that the correct "input" port is being used is important.

With the wide variety of video connector types available, some systems use video adapters to enable the use of slightly mismatched devices. For example, a computer with an HDMI video-out port can be connected to a VGA monitor using an HDMI-to-VGA adapter. The quality and product life of video adapters can vary widely. Therefore, any system with an adapter should have the adapter checked as the possible source of problems.

When the displayed image appears shifted or scaled improperly, the cause can sometimes be an incorrect software display setting on the computer. Both Macintosh and Windows platform computers have a dedicated Display control panel. The control panel should be opened (this is assuming enough of the screen is visible to enable the user to navigate to the Display control panel) and different display profiles and resolutions should be selected to address the problem.

The worst-case scenario for display problems is a hardware problem with the monitor itself, or a hardware problem with the graphics unit on the computer. For desktop computer systems, one way to determine the source of a display problem is to try connecting the questionable components to known working devices. For example, the monitor in question can be connected to a computer that is known to have a working graphics card. If no image is displayed, then the problem is probably with the monitor.

With a monitor hardware problem, replacing the monitor itself may be necessary. For desktop computer systems, this is relatively easy and may just involve a quick trip to a local electronics store. For laptop computer displays can be replaced too, but often require the skills of a computer technician. With graphics card problems, the replacement is complex enough to require the services of a skilled technician.

SUMMARY

Computer peripherals add functionality to existing computer systems. Printers, keyboards, scanners, and monitors are examples of common peripherals. All peripherals send and receive information from a computer, but peripherals can generally be categorized into four main categories: input, output, storage, and communication.

To use any peripheral, some connection hardware must be used with appropriate supporting software. The connection hardware enables a peripheral to send and receive signals from a computer system. The USB standard provides the most commonly used type of physical connection technology. USB 3.0 is the latest standard that provides the fastest communication, but many devices still use the USB 2.0 standard. Other connection standards include FireWire and Thunderbolt. Wireless connections are also an example of a physical connection.

The supporting software, often called a *driver*, acts like a translator for the peripheral and a computer. Each peripheral device has its own specific set of drivers for each computer system. Users rarely interact directly with the drivers. Instead users will interact with application software like a word processor or graphics editor.

When problems occur, usually the connection hardware should be checked first. Sometimes a loose connector simply needs to be reconnected. Other times, there may be software issues that can be checked using a variety of software utilities. Sometimes reinstalling the software will be necessary. Individual peripherals have different particular issues that are unique to that particular type of peripheral. However, the general approach of checking hardware issues first, and software issues second, is still recommended for all peripheral devices.

CASE STUDY

You are a teacher who is using a computer lab for multimedia student projects. The principal has informed you that she can put in a budget request of up to $30,000 for purchasing new equipment for the computer lab and asks you for recommendations. You would like to be able to teach your students to edit and produce video, which would require more high-performance storage and higher quality displays. The lab has thirty desktop computers that are about two years old, equipped with USB 3.0, USB 2.0, FireWire, VGA, and HDMI ports. The teacher computer has the same ports and is currently connected to an old LCD projector with a VGA cable.

Produce a list of peripherals you would recommend to your principal. What kind of storage devices would you recommend and what should their specifications be (connector type, capacity, speed, etc.)? Explain why these choices make sense. What kind of display devices would you recommend and what should their specifications be (display type, connector type, resolution, etc.)? Explain why these choices make sense. What other devices would you recommend and why?

EXERCISES AND DISCUSSION QUESTIONS

1. Describe the main physical connection standards used for most peripheral devices. What are the advantages and disadvantages of each?

2. Name two different types of input devices and two different types of output devices. How do they add value for a user interacting with a computer system?
3. When a device stops functioning as expected, what should be checked first?
4. What is the last resort solution for attempting to fix a software issue?
5. How can the choice of hardware connector influence the performance experienced by a user of a peripheral device like a hard drive or scanner?

REFERENCES

Boettcher, U., Li, H., de Callafon, R., & Talke, F. (2011). Dynamic flying height adjustment in hard disk drives through feed forward control. *IEEE Transactions on Magnetics, 47*(7), 1823–1829.

Mearian, L. (2011). Thunderbolt vs. SuperSpeed USB 3.0. *Computerworld*. Retrieved from http://www.computerworld.com/article/2511551/data-center/thunderbolt-vs--superspeed-usb-3-0.html

Hruska, J. (2014). Next-gen Thunderbolt details: 40Gbps, PCIe 3.0, HDMI 2.0, and 100W power delivery for single-cable PCs. *ExtremeTech*. Retrieved from http://www.extremetech.com/computing/181099-next-gen-thunderbolt-details-40gbps-pcie-3-0-hdmi-2-0-and-100w-power-delivery-for-single-cable-pcs

FOUR

Computer Networking

OBJECTIVES

At the conclusion of this chapter, the reader will be able to:

1. Understand the purpose of network devices and their associated software (ISTE 1, 3).
2. Explain how to implement wired and Wi-Fi networks at schools (ISTE 2, 3, 4).
3. Describe different types of network topologies (ISTE 1, 5).
4. Understand cloud technology and how to access it securely (ISTE 1, 2, 3, 5).
5. Describe the troubleshooting and maintenance of networks (ISTE 3, 4, 5).

NETWORKING OVERVIEW

A computer network is created when two or more computers are connected together to enable them to share data and resources. If additional devices like a printer or a scanner are connected to the network, each computer would then be able to access these additional resources. Computer networking enables the easy sharing of information and resources between computing devices. This easy sharing leads to many benefits for computer users.

The Internet itself is a computer network. It is a very large computer network that spans the entire world, and provides access to vast resources shared by many organizations including companies, universities, libraries, and government agencies. Information from one computer can be sent to a computer on another continent in a matter of seconds. The convenience of this has been experienced by anyone who has spent some time "browsing the web" for research or for fun.

With millions of people attempting to use resources through the Internet at the same time, networking devices and networking rules (or protocols) are needed to help manage the data traffic. Proper management of networking hardware and software is essential for computer networks on both the global scale and the local scale within a classroom or school building.

This chapter discusses the basic concepts behind creating and maintaining computer networks for classrooms and schools. Standard devices needed for creating networks will be discussed, as will the proper arrangement of these devices. Deploying the right hardware with the right software can lead to faster and more reliable computer networks.

BASIC NETWORKING HARDWARE DEVICES

There are three basic hardware devices for creating a computer network. The first device is a computer. Multiple computers are needed to create any computer network. The second required device is a cable or wire. Cables connect computers to each other. Now conceptually, this should be enough to form at least the most basic network. Most computers are equipped with one network port so one computer can be connected to another using a cable.

However, if one wants to form networks of more than two computers, more hardware is needed. An ideal third device would be one that allows other devices to be connected to it, and it would act as a kind of central "hub" that routes information from one computer to another. Every computer could be connected to this "hub" and the hub would enable the computers to communicate with each other.

There is in fact a device called a *hub* that provides this exact service. However, in practice, hubs are rarely used because of some performance limitations of the device. Instead, a more common device used in networks is called a *switch*. It basically does everything a hub does, but allows data to travel between multiple computers much faster.

Another type of device that basically takes a switch and adds some network managing capabilities to it is called a *router*. Routers provide network administrative features that allow more flexible configuring of small and large networks. Finally, a wireless router does everything a router does but adds the ability to create wireless network connections.

In summary, the three types of devices needed to form a basic computer network of more than two computers are (1) computers, (2) cables, and (3) a central "hub" device. In modern computer network situations, a wireless router is usually chosen for the central hub. This then also allows computers to connect to the network using the cables or using a wireless connection.

NETWORK TOPOLOGIES

The way that computers are connected to each other in a network is called *network topology*. The typical computer user does not care what network topology was set up by the information technology (IT) people. A user simply wants to have fast and reliable access to local resources (like the printer and file server) and to global resources (like the World Wide Web).

However, the choice of network topology can influence a user's experience. The topology determines how efficiently and reliably data is processed and routed on a computer network. For a person participating in the design and implementation of a new computer network, understanding the various topologies can be very helpful.

There are six basic types of network topologies: bus, mesh, ring, star, tree, and hybrid. Each topology has a different design to connect computers in a network. Cost and reliability are the major issues associated with these topologies.

In a bus network topology, the components are lined up on both sides of a path. Extra computers or devices can be added and the cable can be extended from both ends. When the cable line is severed, the computers at the end of the severed line cannot access the server. Figure 4.1 shows that the server is in the middle and the printer is at the end. If there is a breach in the cable line between the server and the printer, then the print command cannot be transmitted.

In a mesh network topology, computers are all interconnected. This topology is very reliable, but running wires among computers over long distances can be costly. Mesh topology is useful in a free-standing localized area. Figure 4.2 shows a mesh network topology consisting of several computers, a printer, and a server interconnected with extensive wiring.

In a ring network topology, cables transport data through the computers and through each other until the data reach their intended destinations. For example, if the user's computer is next to the server and the user wants to print data, the information needs to travel to the server first. Then the data are transmitted through all the other computers to reach the printer (figure 4.3). This process causes delays because of excessive traffic. If there is a breakdown of a computer in the ring, communication in the network is not possible.

In a star network topology, all the computers are connected to a hub in a star fashion (figure 4.4). A hub is a network device that connects several computers through its ports. The network administrator can add or dis-

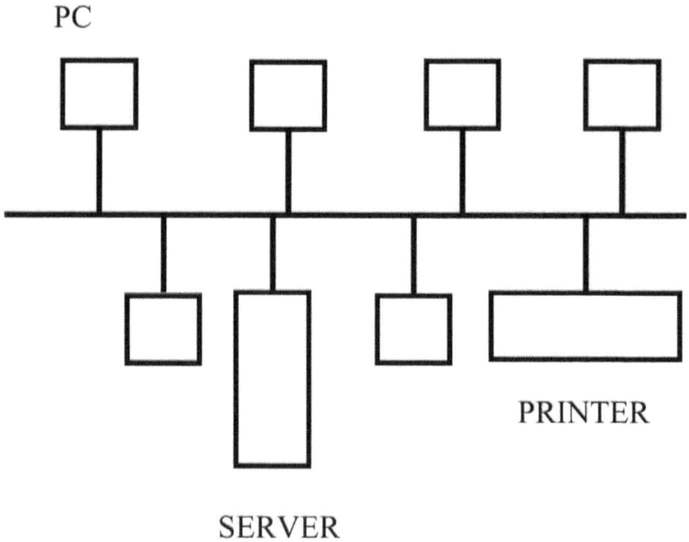

Figure 4.1. Bus network topology.

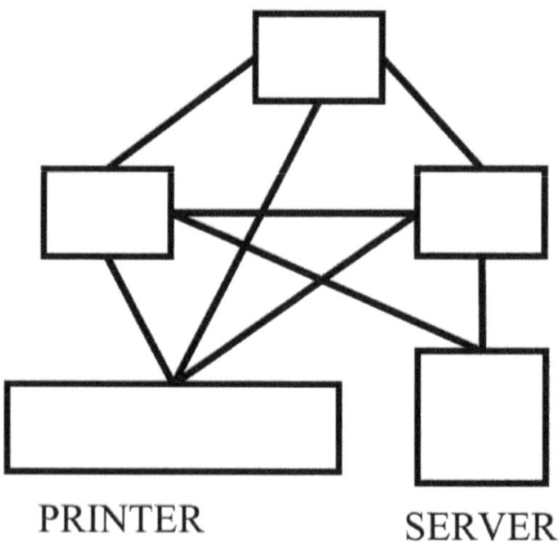

Figure 4.2. Mesh network topology.

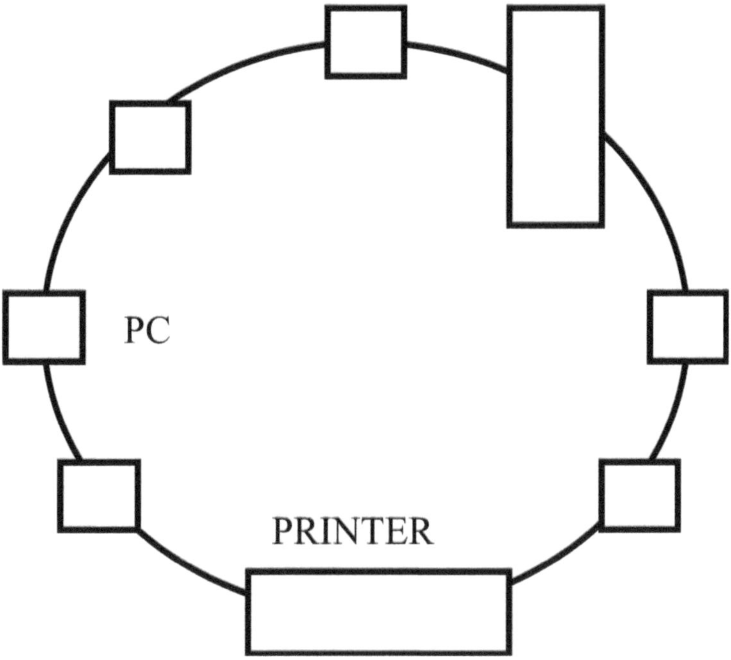

Figure 4.3. Ring network topology.

connect a computer easily without disturbing the rest of the star network. All computers are connected through the hub. The disadvantage of the star topology is that when the hub is not functioning, the computers in the star topology are unable to communicate.

In a tree network topology all the computers are connected like branches of a tree (figure 4.5). The computers on the same branch are connected to a hub on the trunk. The network administrator can add computers easily to any branch. Also, new branches can be added to the tree by adding hubs to the trunk. The disadvantage of the tree topology is that when a hub stops working, all the computers connected to that hub lose connectivity.

A hybrid network topology is a combination of network topologies. There can be several cable lines with different technologies, all connected to the backbone through hubs or bridges, as shown in figure 4.6. A bridge is a network device that segments large networks into smaller networks.

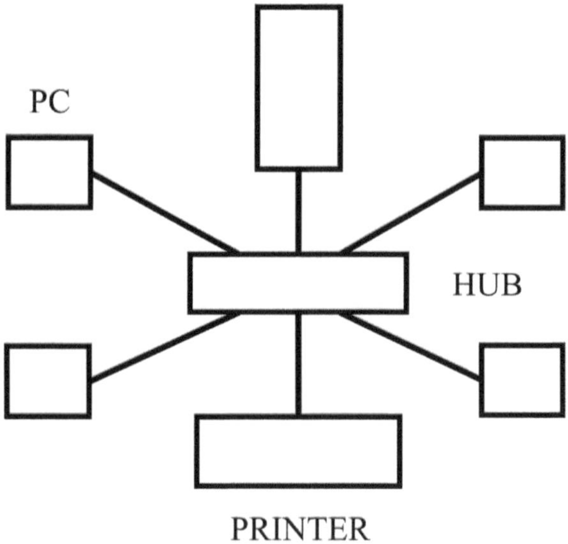

Figure 4.4. Star network topology.

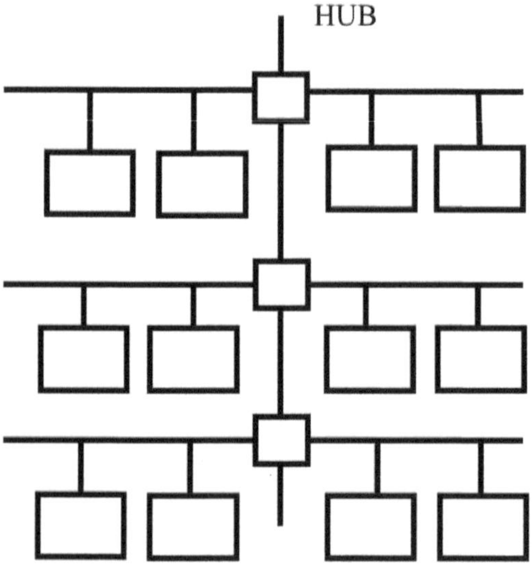

Figure 4.5. Tree network topology.

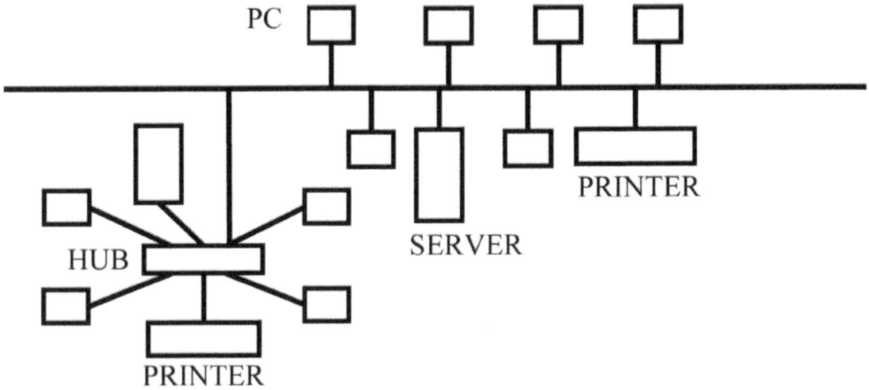

Figure 4.6. Hybrid network topology.

Hybrid topology offers reliability and increases the fault tolerance as compared with other topologies.

ADDITIONAL NETWORKING DEVICES AND SOFTWARE

A basic computer network and the required devices were described in an earlier section of this chapter. In this section, more advanced devices and their functions are explained. An understanding of these advanced devices will enable a user to create more powerful computer networks.

Computers, laptops, and other wireless devices such as iPhones and iPads are connected to the Internet through local, metropolitan, and wide area networks. Local area networks (LAN) can cover a room, a building on a campus, or an entire school. Metropolitan area networks (MAN) cover a town, city, or other metropolitan area. Wide area networks (WAN) cover cities, countries, and the globe.

Network devices such as repeaters, hubs, bridges, switches, and routers interconnect the LANs, MANs, and WANs together throughout the world. Every network device has a specific purpose. All network devices are designed to help extend the traveling distances of the signals. Communication signals travel through wireless towers. Copper, Ethernet, and fiber-optic cables are needed to transmit signals to their destinations. Network congestion problems are minimized with the use of repeaters, hubs, bridges, switches, and routers.

Repeaters are used to eliminate and clean electrical noise from the transmitted or received signals in the LANs. Repeaters clean the noise as signals are transmitted through cables and wireless devices. Once the noise is cleaned up, repeaters regenerate the data and send them to the

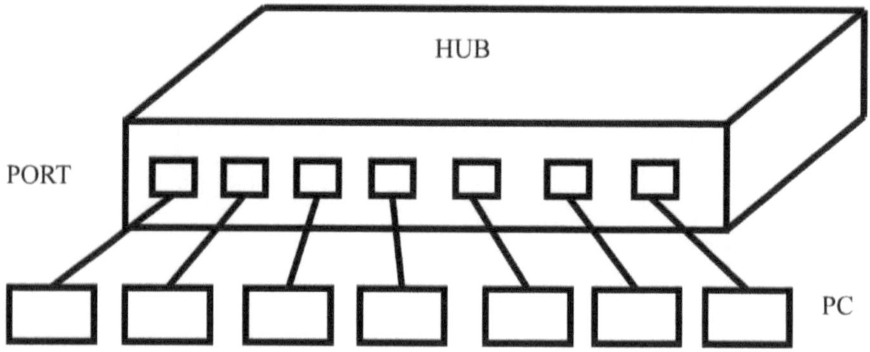

Figure 4.7. Back view of a hub.

communication towers. The clean signals are then sent to the destination networks. Each repeater has one incoming port and one outgoing port.

Hubs are network devices that regenerate signals and operate in LANs. Figure 4.7 shows the back view of a hub with seven ports connected to seven computers. Unlike repeaters, hubs have multiple ports. Hubs are used in star, tree, and hybrid topologies. Once the data arrives at one of the ports, the hub copies the information to the rest of the ports for other segments of the LAN to access.

A bridge is a network device that has two ports. It is used in large networks, and it segments a large LAN into two small networks. Segmenting or separating a large LAN network into two small networks reduces network traffic problems. Traffic issues within one LAN do not affect the flow of data in the second LAN. As a result, speed and efficiency of data transfer increase. Figure 4.8 illustrates a bridge connecting two LANs.

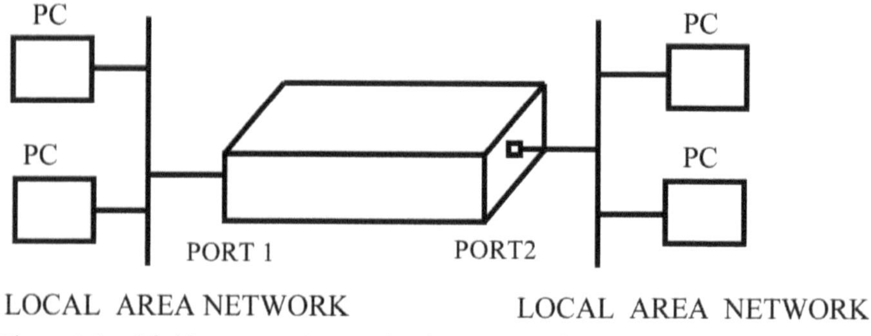

Figure 4.8. A bridge connecting two local area networks.

Bridges also create separate collision domains. Collisions occur when more than one computer tries to transmit within a LAN at the same time, which causes traffic and time delays. The computers within a LAN that are affected form a collision domain through one of the two ports of the bridge. After a collision occurs, each computer has to retransmit data. Computers retransmit data one at a time, within a time frame, decided by a software program called a *back-off algorithm* (Dye, 2014).

Bridges are used to minimize the traffic delays caused by collisions. Because the bridge segments the large network into two LANs, the collision problems occurring in one LAN do not affect the other LAN. Therefore, traffic delays due to collisions occur in one LAN and yet the second LAN can operate normally without any delays.

Switches operate in LANs, MANs, WANs, and they have multiple ports. Figure 4.9 shows the back of a twenty-four-port switch (connected to six computers), which acts like a multiport bridge. Switches are more expensive than bridges, hubs, and repeaters. The bandwidth and data transmission rate remain constant for every computer connected to a switch port. Switches maintain the transmission rates through the computers. Hubs and repeaters reduce the data transmission rates depending on the number of computers connected to the ports.

In a switch, each port can connect to a small network. Through segmentation of the network into several small LANs, switches create separate collision domains. Segmentation reduces traffic and increases data transmission rates. With the connection of a computer to a switch by a console

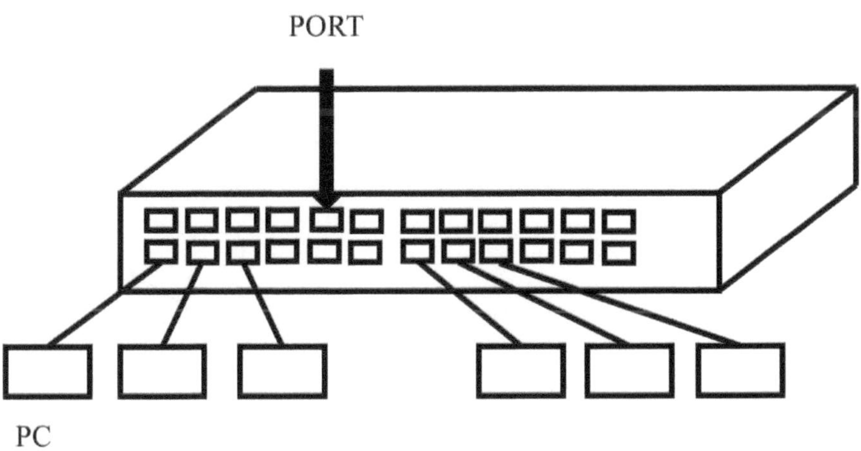

Figure 4.9. A bridge connecting two local area networks.

cable, the network administrator can install the Internetwork Operating System (IOS) software for the switch.

After the installation of IOS software, the IT department connects the switch to the computers in the classroom or the lab. The switch then creates a table that contains the media access control (MAC) addresses of computers connected to all its ports (Lewis, 2012). Each computer has its own unique MAC address. After the data arrive, the switch looks at its MAC address table. Through the MAC address table, the switch knows which port to forward the data through to reach the correct computer.

Routers are network devices that connect LANs, MANs, and WANs. They each have Ethernet ports that connect to the computers in the LAN. They also have WAN ports that connect to routers in other LANs, MANs, or WANs. Figure 4.10 illustrates the back view of a router. Routers perform functions to construct routing tables. Through the routing tables, routers send and receive data through their appropriate ports. Routers are more expensive than switches and data processing rates are lower in routers than switches.

In each network, network devices and computers have their own unique Internet protocol (IP) addresses. The router builds the routing table, which contains the IP addresses of the computers, devices, and networks directly connected to the router. Also, the routing table has a corresponding router port name next to each IP address. The router updates the routing tables each time the network administrator adds a new computer to the network or disconnects a computer from the network.

For example, when a data packet that contains 1500 bytes to 2000 bytes arrives at the router from the transmitting computer, the router looks at the tag that the transmitting computer delivers. This tag includes the destination computer's IP address. The router then looks up the destination IP address in the routing table. As soon as the router finds the IP address

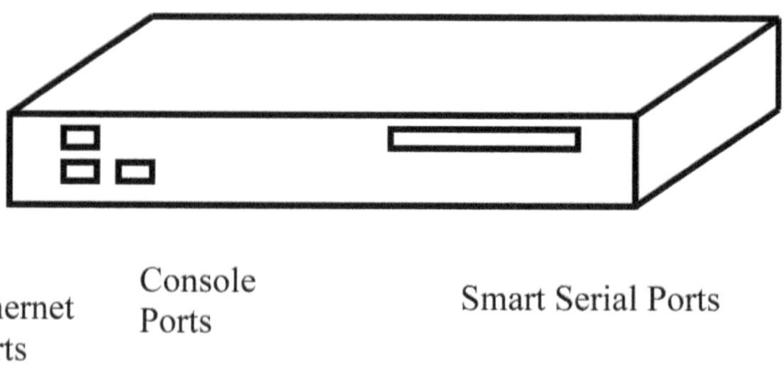

Figure 4.10. Back view of a router.

and the corresponding port name, it sends the packets out to its appropriate port to the destination computer (Tomal & Agajanian, 2014). This process is called *path determination*.

In a router, each Ethernet LAN port represents a collision domain just like in a switch. Because a large LAN network is divided into small collision domains, traffic is reduced. A router also increases data transmission rates by creating broadcast domains through each one of the ports. Broadcast occurs when a computer sends data to all computers within the broadcast domain of the router. Increasing the number of broadcast domains through multiple ports of the router helps reduce traffic congestions.

Routers and switches operate with the IOS software just like computers operate with the OS software. Once the IT department installs the IOS to the router through a computer, the user can program the router by using the commands through the command line interface (CLI). With the use of router commands, the user can set the router's name, setup IP addresses of the ports or interfaces, apply protocols for different ways of routing packets, and enter passwords. Passwords are needed so that hackers are not able to access the private networks.

CLOUD TECHNOLOGY AND SECURITY

Cloud technology refers to groups of computers that store data and provide resources or services to individual users. A computer that primarily provides services is usually called a *server*. "The cloud" is a general term that means the service is provided by some remote group of servers that may be run by companies like Google or Microsoft. Any computer can store data on the cloud by accessing the servers through a web browser. Cloud computing is the process of accessing software to complete certain data processing tasks (Palaniappan, 2014).

Traditionally, users have stored data locally with the use of USB flash drives, CDs, internal and external hard drives, DVDs, emails, and so on. Through cloud storage, users are able to access the data at any place and time. Cloud storage can also give users the opportunity to store large amounts of data at a nominal cost. Storage companies provide secure and reliable services to store and access data for the customers.

Through the cloud, the user can access the software he or she needs to implement a job at a minimal cost. Software installed in multiple computers increases the cost of licensing. To circumvent this problem, users of cloud services do not need to have software locally licensed. Instead they can perform their work in the cloud.

Cloud technology allows users to upload or download documents and edit and share them. For privacy, uploaders have the option of allowing certain other users to share their documents. There are a multitude of cloud technology services for storing and sharing music, video, and photos. Through email on cloud servers, we are able to communicate privately for free. There are also social media cloud applications for specific interest groups.

Some of the advantages of cloud technology include saving hardware space, lowering costs, and reducing the need for IT support. The disadvantage of cloud technologies is that the system can be slow. Slow access is due to a large number of users trying to access cloud services at the same time. Cloud storage companies are trying to improve network bandwidth for data, video, and voice transmission.

Security and privacy are two concerns related to cloud technology. Companies who own the cloud servers are careful to use all appropriate security and privacy measures to provide high-quality service. As a precaution, clients of cloud services should back up their data through secondary local storage as well. Implementing the following guidelines helps improve security when using cloud access:

1. Choose smart passwords by entering a combination of numbers, letters, and symbols or alphanumeric characters, including upper- and lowercase letters. Create a password that is hard for anyone to guess.
2. Don't use the same passwords for different services. For example, if the same password is used for all sites, and a hacker accesses a user's email account, then the hacker might be able to access all the other accounts as well.
3. Besides storing data in the cloud, always back up data in secondary storage devices such as USB flash drive, hard drive, CD, DVD, email, or other physical storage device.
4. Use software that saves a user's passwords under a master password. To protect all the other passwords, the master password should be very unpredictable, long, and impossible to guess.
5. Be aware of the surroundings, including where a computer is being used. When logging into the computer, make sure nobody is watching while entering the user ID and the password. Do not leave the computer unattended. Logout or lock a computer before leaving.
6. Use personal hot spots instead of a free Wi-Fi connection to maximize security of computers, laptops, or devices.

CREATING NETWORKS IN SCHOOLS

The following questions need to be answered before any design plans are created: How many computers are going to be connected in the network in each room? How many rooms are there per floor? How many floors are there in the building? How many buildings are there? What kind of future expansion is expected for each room and building? What kind of routers will be installed: wireless or wired? Appropriate answers to these questions minimize future complications.

Then a series of steps can be followed to design appropriate networks for schools. First the designer has to assess the space or spaces receiving a network. For example, laboratory rooms require different software and hardware than the regular classrooms and offices. The designer also needs to know the budget and make plans accordingly.

The next step is to determine number of servers and network devices. Network devices include hubs, switches, and routers (wired or wireless). A server is a dedicated computer that filters out Internet traffic for the LAN. Also, the users share applications and resources faster and more efficiently among the LAN computers through proper server management.

Depending on the number of computers in a specific room, a server might be needed to provide fast Internet access. As the number of computers increase in the network, the information access time decreases per computer. When a server is connected to a network, information access and transfer times decrease.

For example, for the network administrator, using a 48-port Cisco switch in a classroom or lab of forty-four computers is the optimal solution to reduce the network traffic problems. With the use of switches, the bandwidth becomes greater and Internet access will be faster for each computer. However, switches are more expensive than hubs. Therefore, having a hub in each classroom is the next best solution for limited budgets.

All networks need routers that process data, voice, or video packets efficiently. If a wireless router is used, the network administrator needs to make sure that the computers have wireless network adapters. These adapters have to have standards that are compatible with the routers. Please see the section in this chapter titled "Instructions to Install a Wireless or Wi-Fi Router."

Instructions to Connect Wired Routers

Figure 4.11 shows typical router connections to an LAN. When the data travel from the cloud to the local network, they arrive at the router first. The router looks at the IP address of the packets of data and routes them out to the appropriate port connected to the server. The server then transmits the data to the switch, and the switch sends it out of its ports to the appropriate computers.

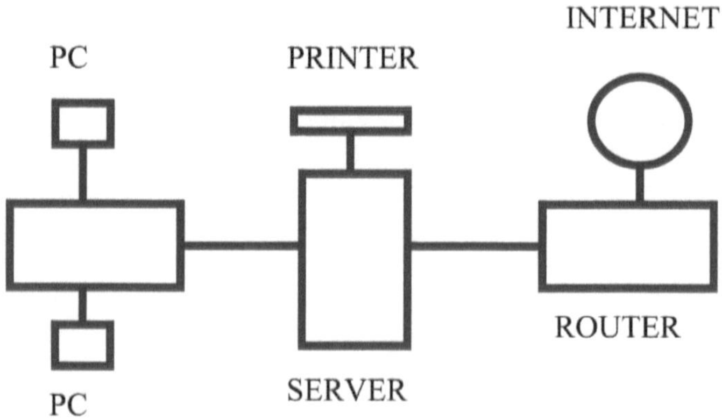

Figure 4.11. Diagram of router connections to a local area network.

To install a network in a lab or classroom in a school, the network administrator needs to determine which cables, software, computers, servers, routers, switches, and printers are optimal. It is very important to install the router close to the Internet service provider's (ISP) connection to maximize the flow of information. The network administrator should connect all of the Ethernet cables from each computer to one of the switch ports. Ethernet cables should be used also to connect the switch to the server, and also from the server to the router.

The following steps summarize the procedures to implement connectivity between router, switch, and the computers, including hardware and software:

1. Plug the router into the wall. Turn on the power switch. To have a high-speed Internet connection, connect the Ethernet port on the back of the router to the digital subscriber line (DSL) or cable modem's Ethernet port.
2. Connect the router to the switch through an Ethernet cable. Connect each of the switch's Ethernet ports individually to a computer's Ethernet port.
3. When the switch, router, and all the computers are powered up, the green light-emitting diodes (LEDs) light up on the switch, router, and all the computer's LAN ports. If any of the green LEDs fail to

light up, refer to the "Check TCP/IP Settings" and "Check Client Applications" topics under the "Network Troubleshooting" section of this chapter.

General Instructions for Installing a Wireless or Wi-Fi Router

To set up wireless routers, apply the following general steps:

1. Consult the device manual to determine the wireless standard used by the router.
2. Follow the router connections to laptops and computers shown in figure 4.12. The modem should be connected to the Internet through a coaxial cable. An Ethernet cable should connect the WAN port of the router to the modem. The router and the wireless access point (WAP) also need to connect through an Ethernet cable.
3. Login with the user ID and the password to the WAP provided by the router's user manual. After the login, change the service set identifier (SSID) of the router to make sure the network is secure. Only users who have access permission are able to communicate with the network.

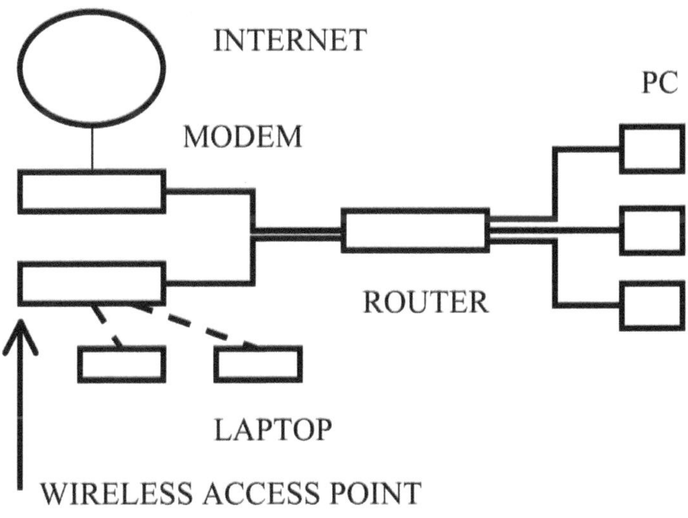

Figure 4.12. Diagram of router connections to laptops and computers.

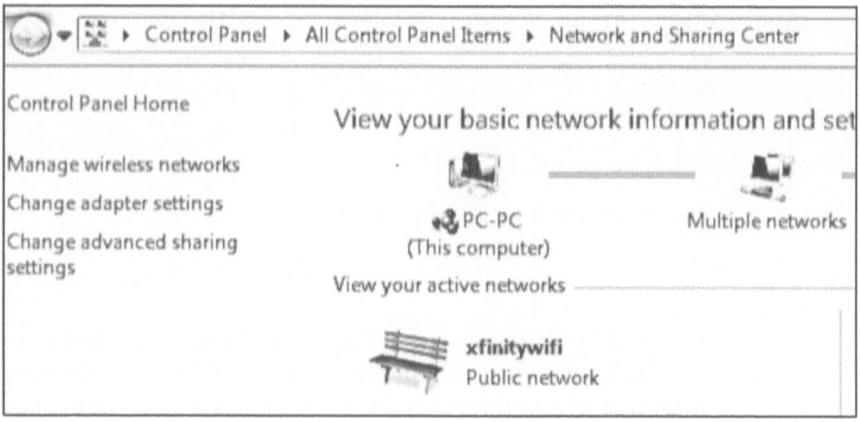

Figure 4.13. An example of a screen shot to install a wireless router.

4. All new computers are built with wireless adapters or wireless network interface cards (WNIC). If the WNIC is missing, it can be purchased and installed. Follow the directions provided by the manufacturer. Make sure the wireless adapter is compatible with the computer.

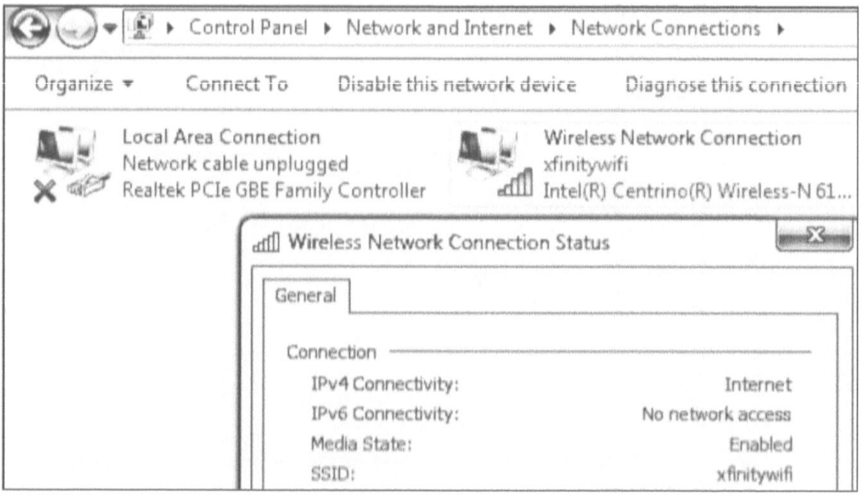

Figure 4.14. An example of a screen shot to install a wireless router.

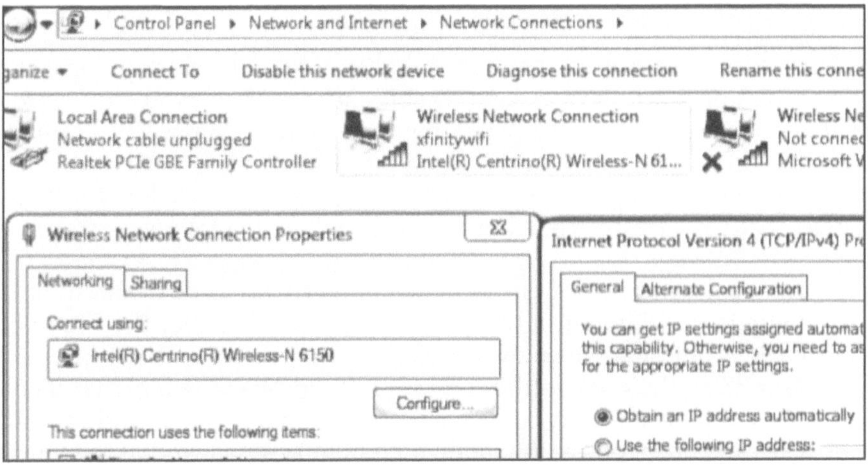

Figure 4.15. An example of a screen shot to install a wireless router.

5. Figures 4.13, 4.14, and 4.15 show the screenshots for installing a wireless router with a Windows computer. As shown in figure 4.13, click "Control Panel," "Network and Sharing Center," and "Change Adapter Settings."
6. Double-click the Network Connection that the LAN is connected to. For example, double-click "Wireless Network Connection xfinity-wifi" as shown in figure 4.14.
7. As shown in figure 4.15, double-click "Properties" and then "Internet Protocol Version 4 (TCP/IP/IPv4)." Make sure the Properties are set as follows: "Obtain an IP address automatically and Obtain DNS server address automatically."
8. Repeat step 7 for Internet Protocol Version 6 (TCP/IP/IPv6).

TROUBLESHOOTING NETWORKS AND MAINTENANCE

The best way to troubleshoot a network is to check the hardware issues first, test for software problems next, and if necessary check client application settings. The network administrator should turn on the power for the hardware. If there are no problems with the hardware, the network administrator should install and troubleshoot all the software needed for the network. As the last step, the network administrator should check client application issues by setting the appropriate security levels for the computers, router, and switch.

Troubleshooting Hardware Problems

Hardware problems can be related to the cable connections at the computers and network devices. Loose cables are common problems. Hardware problems also could involve the operation of computers, routers, switches, hubs, and modems. For example, while trying to access the Internet, if the "webpage is not accessible" message is received on the computer, check hardware-related problems by taking the following steps:

1. Check the indicator light at the computer's network connection. If there is no blinking light, the problem could be that the Ethernet cable is not plugged in correctly.
2. Reconnect the cable at the computer. If a problem still exists, check the lights at the port connections for the hub, router, and switch. Check connections at the modem and the WAP as well. If the lights of the network device turn on, then try to access the Internet again. If the connection fails, check the computer's Ethernet connection and skip to step 4.
3. If the light is still off at a network device, check the device's power switch. If the power switch is off, turn it on. If the network device does not turn on, troubleshoot the device by consulting the users' manual. If necessary, replace the device. When the device power is on, then test the cables with a cable tester. If the cables do not test according to their specifications, replace them with new ones. If the cables test according to specifications, proceed to the next step.
4. Check to see if the network interface card (NIC) card is properly installed at the correct expansion slot and check if the indicator light is on. If the light is on, continue with step 5. If not, reinsert the NIC card at the appropriate expansion slot and proceed to the next step.
5. On a Windows computer, click on the "Device Manager" under "Control Panel" in the computer to check the NIC card. Log onto the NIC card's manufacturer's website. Uninstall the device drivers and reinstall them with their new updates.
6. After updating the device drivers, access the Internet again. If the Internet is still not accessible, replace the NIC card. Make sure the NIC card is compatible with the network speed. Check the indicator light at the NIC card and connect to the Internet. If Internet access is still unsuccessful, proceed with the next section.

Troubleshooting Software Problems

Software problems are associated with transmission control protocol/ Internet protocol (TCP/IP) network address settings for the computers and network devices, and compatibility of device IOS with the computer OS. To test the connectivity, TCP/IP settings need to be checked. Follow these steps to achieve an Internet connection on a Windows computer:

1. Type *ipconfig/release* and *ipconfig/renew* in the command prompt. A new IP address will be assigned to the computer.
2. Enter *ipconfig/all* in the command prompt. Observe the IP address, subnet mask, default gateway, and MAC address of the computer. Make sure "DHCP Enabled" is on. If it is not on, the computer cannot access the dynamic host configuration protocol (DHCP) server. If the DHCP server is not reachable, the computer cannot receive an IP address. Without an IP address, the computer cannot connect to the Internet.
3. Enter the loopback address ping 127.0.0.1 for IPv4, or ping ::1 for IPv6 in the command prompt interface of the computer. With this diagnostics test, the user knows if the computer's IP address works properly. Proceed to step 5.
4. If this diagnostic test fails, then the network administrator should manage TCP/IP settings manually. Enter "ipconfig/all" in the command prompt; record the IP address, subnet mask, and gateway IP address of the computer.
5. Follow the steps to troubleshoot software problems on a Windows computer as shown in figure 4.16.
6. Attempt to access the Internet. If there is no connectivity, recheck the connections of the router to the Internet as follows:
   a. Turn off the modem and the router.
   b. Turn the modem and the router back on. Observe until the lights turn on.

1) Left click control panel "Network and internet."
2) Left click "View network status and tasks."
3) Left click "Change adapter settings."
4) Right click "Wireless network connection" or "Local area connection."
5) Left click "Properties."
6) Double click "Internet protocol v4."
7) Left click "Properties."
8) Left click "Use the following address."
9) Type the IP address, subnet mask, default gateway address.
10) Close the "Properties" box.
11) Close the "Network connection" box.

Figure 4.16. Examples of steps to troubleshoot software problems.

7. If the router is not working, disconnect and reconnect the router.
8. If there is still no Internet access, then proceed with the next section.

Troubleshooting Client Applications

Firewall, email protocol, file transfer protocol (FTP), and voice over IP (VoIP) settings can all be the problems related to client applications (Andrews, 2014). Security settings of a router should allow communication with the Internet. The information coming from the Internet can pass or stop at the router according to the firewall settings. Setting firewall, antivirus, and antimalware correctly prevents the malicious software or hackers from accessing the computer systems. As a result, the network connectivity to the Internet is improved.

As shown in figure 4.17 for a Windows computer, following the steps is important to ensure the correct firewall settings. After setting the firewall, if connection to the Internet is still impossible, then the proxy server might be the problem. A proxy server, sometimes called a *gateway,* allows the client to access the Internet by going through a different web browser. One of the main tasks of the network administrator is to assign the correct proxy server and provide secure connections. Proxy servers provide faster Internet access by filtering out the excess traffic.

Setting up email post office protocol (POP) and simple mail transfer protocol (SMTP) on the computer by checking the ISP's website also eases up the Internet mail access. FTP is used for large file transfers by entering

1) Left click "Start."
2) Left click "Control panel."
3) Left click "System and security."
4) Left click "Windows firewall."
5) Left click "Change notification settings."
6) Turn windows firewall on.
7) Left click "Notify me when windows firewall blocks a new program."
8) Left click "OK."
9) Left click "Use recommended settings."
10) Left click "Restore defaults."
11) Left click "Yes."

Figure 4.17. Step-by-step instructions for firewall settings.

ftp instead of *http* at the Internet address line. If the FTP site is not reachable, try the following steps:

1. Contact the network administrator to receive permission to access the FTP site.
2. Ask the network administrator to add ports 20, 21 to the firewall.
3. Check connectivity with the FTP server by pinging to the server's IP address.

Network Maintenance

Network maintenance consists of checking both hardware and software. Preventive hardware maintenance includes inspection of routers, switches, other network devices, computers, cables, and memory cards. The IT department of the school needs to check the random access memory (RAM) cards frequently. For software maintenance, the network administrator needs to update IOS software for routers and switches every time a new version is available. The updated versions of the IOS software require additional RAM.

The healthy operation of a network depends on routine checks. Entering errors and problems into event logs when necessary ensures proper maintenance of the networks. Inspecting wiring closets and fixing errors are among the follow-up activities. The following items summarize most of the routine preventive maintenance tasks that the IT department needs to perform on the computers for fast, efficient, and trouble-free operations:

1. Turn on the Firewall.
2. Install and automatically update antimalware and antivirus programs. These programs clean up viruses, worms, Trojan horses, and spyware that cause problems in computer operations.
3. Set the computer to install operating system updates automatically.
4. Defragment the hard drive. This process speeds up computer performance.
5. Take security measures by changing network access passwords frequently.
6. Repair the file system errors by using an appropriate disk utility.
7. Use "Add and Remove Programs" to remove the unwanted programs. This process also creates more memory space in the hard drive.
8. Follow up any unauthorized attempt to access the computer by observing "Administrative Tools" and "View Event Logs."
9. Document all issues and their resolutions by keeping a reasonable maintenance schedule.

10. Monitor CPU and memory utilization with efficient management of files and folders.
11. Keep the print heads of the printers clean. Dust computers, hubs, switches, routers, screens, and keyboards.
12. Document all new computer, device, and network accessory purchases. Report any unused network components.

SUMMARY

Computer networking is basically two or more computers or devices sharing the same data and resources. Networks communicate to each other and have several different purposes. The way that computers are connected to each other in a network is called *network topology*.

There are six basic types of network topologies: bus, mesh, ring, star, tree, and hybrid. Cost and reliability are the major issues that separate the topologies. Computers, laptops, and other wireless devices such as iPhones and iPads are connected to the Internet through local, metropolitan, and wide area networks. LANs cover a room, building on a campus, or a company. MANs cover a town, city, and metropolitan area computers. WANs cover cities, countries, and the globe.

Cloud technology refers to services delivered through the Internet by a third-party company. Any computer can connect to the cloud services through a web browser to store data or perform cloud-based computing tasks.

Designing networks in schools requires following certain steps in a particular order. First, the designer has to assess the rooms receiving networks. For example, laboratory rooms require different software and hardware than the regular classrooms. To install the network in a lab or classroom at a school, the network administrator needs to gather all the data about the cables, software, computers, servers, routers, switches, and printers before purchasing.

The best way to troubleshoot a network is to check the hardware issues first, test for software problems next, and finally if necessary check client application settings. The hardware problems relate to cables; connections at the computers or network devices; and the operation of computers, routers, switches, hubs, and modems. Software problems are associated with TCP/IP network address settings for the computers and network devices and compatibility of the device IOS with the computer OS.

CASE STUDY

You are in charge of designing a computer network for forty students at your school. You have been asked to consider various network topologies. Describe how you might go about selecting the components, equipment, and supplies needed to install your top two choices. List the advantages and disadvantages of each of these network topologies. Also, include a chart or table listing the differences in these networks and resources needed for the maintenance and continued operation.

EXERCISES AND DISCUSSION QUESTIONS

1. List and describe the six basic types of network topologies. Include the advantages and disadvantages of each. Include a chart listing these differences.
2. Describe cloud technology.
3. Describe the overall design of a typical network in a school. Explain the needed resources for the network, including hardware, software, security, and maintenance issues.
4. What are some of the common faults of a network? Describe typical troubleshooting techniques for hardware and software issues.
5. What are hubs, bridges, routers, and switches? What functions do they perform and why are they needed? Explain.

REFERENCES

Andrews, J. (2014). *A+ guide to managing and maintaining your PC*. Boston, MA: Course Technology.

Dye, M. (2014). *Switched networks companion guide.* Indianapolis: Cisco.

Palaniappan, S. (2014). Cloud computing for academic environment. *International Journal of Computer Science and Mobile Computing,* 3(5), 8–15.

Tomal, D., and Agajanian, A. (2014). *Electronic troubleshooting.* New York: McGraw-Hill.

FIVE

Computing Platforms for Schools

OBJECTIVES

At the conclusion of the chapter, the reader will be able to:

1. Explain what a computing platform is (ISTE 1, 3, 6).
2. Identify the main computing platforms used by schools (ISTE 1, 3, 6).
3. Describe the main advantages of each platform (ISTE 1, 2, 3, 6).
4. Justify the choice of various platforms for common sets of school tasks (ISTE 1, 2, 3, 5, 6).
5. Explain the tradeoffs that must be considered when considering platforms for an existing school computing infrastructure (ISTE 1, 2, 3, 5, 6).

OVERVIEW OF COMPUTING PLATFORMS

What are computing platforms? Which computing platforms are best suited for schools? What are the strengths and weaknesses of each platform? How does one go about deciding which platform to buy? A computing platform (or computer platform) generally means some computing hardware running some operating system software. Examples of computing platforms include a "Dell Inspiron desktop computer running the Windows 8 operating system" and an "Apple MacBook laptop computer running the MacOS X operating system" (see figure 5.1).

Computing platforms also come in much smaller sizes. A "Samsung Galaxy Tablet running the Android operating system" and an "Apple iPhone running the iOS operating system" are also examples of computing platforms. For convenience, short phrases like the "Mac platform" and the "Windows platform" are often used as well. These references are more general and include all hardware configurations running the MacOS X operating system or all hardware configurations running the latest Windows operating system, respectively.

Figure 5.1. Examples of desktop and laptop computing platforms. (Courtesy Dell Inc. and Apple Inc.)

Computing platforms usually have a set of rules and specifications that must be followed so that software developers can write programs (or "apps") for the platforms. Developers often create multiple versions of their software to run on different platforms. For example, Microsoft Word has versions for both the Windows and MacOS X operating system platforms. The Chrome web browser has versions for the Windows, MacOS X, Android, iOS, and other operating system platforms.

Computing platforms also offer devices available in a broad range of physical shapes and sizes. When trying to select a device to use for a certain task, there are often many options that will work. For example, if a computing device is needed for conducting web research, almost any computing platform can provide access to the web for basic searching. However, different devices will offer varying levels of convenience and speed.

This chapter continues with a description of the primary dimensions that should be considered when comparing computing platforms. Following that, the characteristics of computing devices in three popular physical form categories—(1) desktops, (2) laptops, and (3) tablets—are compared and discussed in greater detail. Their ability to perform common school tasks will also be considered. Developing an understanding of the tradeoffs various computing platform options provide can help a person make cost-effective choices for different school and work situations.

PRIMARY COMPARISON FACTORS

When comparing computing platform options, several factors should be considered. They can be grouped under three main categories:

1. Physical functionality
2. Computational functionality
3. Cost

Physical Functionality

When trying to choose a platform for a particular school task, the physical properties of a computing device and the functionality enabled by these physical properties are very important considerations. For example, if computers are needed for the school's automotive shop program, portability and durability may be important. If computers are needed for the school's visual arts program, large displays and expandability may be important. Among the more important physical properties for computers are the following:

- Device size
- Device weight
- Screen size
- User input options
- Physical build quality
- Upgradability

When considering *device size and weight,* generally speaking, computers can be anywhere on a spectrum that goes from very large and heavy to very small and light. On the large and heavy side, there are desktop computers, which should be secured on top of desks and should not be moved around very much. On the small and light side, there are mobile devices like smartphones and tablet computers that can be carried around easily. In between there are laptops, which provide portability with computational power comparable to desktops. Figure 5.2 illustrates different sizes of computers.

The physical size differences in turn influence the way users interact with the devices. The larger desktops and laptops are able to provide larger screens, which make viewing text and images easier. Some types of user input, like typed text, are easier to enter when using a full-sized keyboard compared to a small touch-screen keyboard.

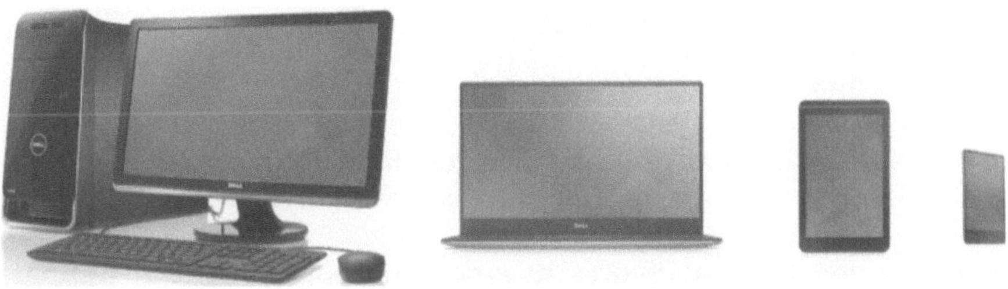

Figure 5.2. Examples of sizes of computing platforms. (Courtesy Dell Inc.)

Physical build quality is not necessarily connected to physical size. There are solidly constructed desktop computers as well as poorly constructed desktop computers. There are solidly constructed mobile devices as well as poorly constructed mobile devices. Mobile devices with good physical build quality are more likely to survive bumps and minor drops. Any physical device with poor physical build quality will not last very long under heavy use in a school setting, so this factor is something that needs to be considered.

Upgradability is another important feature when considering the service life of a computing device. Devices that can be upgraded with more memory, faster processors, or higher capacity batteries tend to have a longer useful lifecycle. Desktop computers are usually built with easy-to-access physical compartments to enable fairly easy upgrades. They are also typically equipped with several external ports to enable connection to a large number of peripheral devices.

Laptop computers are usually constructed with reasonable access to common components like internal hard drives and random access memory (RAM) to allow some upgradability. They are also usually equipped with at least one universal serial bus (USB) port to enable connection to peripheral devices. Mobile devices like tablets and smartphones are typically not designed to permit user upgrades of internal components. All have at least one port to connect to peripherals, but the operating systems of mobile devices typically do not permit the flexible use of peripherals one would expect with desktop and laptop platforms.

Computational Functionality

The computational properties of a computing device are another important dimension to consider when trying to choose a platform for a particular school task. Among the more important computational properties are the following:

- Processing power
- Software tools and applications availability and usability
- User interface
- Network connectivity
- Operating system
- Personal data ecosystem
- Peripheral device availability and compatibility
- Existing technology infrastructure compatibility

Not only are there differences in processing power between computing platforms, there are also differences within a computing platform.

For example, in most cases, desktop computers provide the fastest raw processing speed while mobile devices provide the slowest raw processing speed. However, within the desktop physical form family, some are very fast while others are considerably slower. In fact, many higher end laptops have more processing power than lower end desktop computers.

A computing platform should be chosen based on the processing needs of the task to be performed. For example, if simple note taking or text editing is all that is needed, not much processing power is required. However, if complex science simulations need to be run or digital video needs to be edited, a lot of processing power will be needed.

If processing power is sufficient, it is important to consider whether the appropriate software tools or apps will be available for the target task. For example, a school newspaper editor may need to view and comment on articles submitted by student reporters in Word, PDF, and RTF format. When selecting a computing device for the newspaper editor, it is important to choose a platform that has programs that will allow the editor to easily open and add comments to Word, PDF, and RTF format files.

The user interface is an important property, and it was a focal point in the epic rivalry between Apple and Microsoft platforms. This rivalry is sometimes referred to as the "Mac vs. PC" rivalry or more recently, the "Mac vs. Windows" rivalry. Briefly, the original Macintosh computer was introduced in 1984 and was the first mass-market computer to rely primarily on a graphical user interface (GUI). Microsoft, in an attempt to catch up, licensed parts of the Mac GUI and introduced its Windows 1.0 operating system in 1985.

Subsequent versions of Windows imitated more and more of the Mac GUI, leading to a lawsuit over user interface elements and "look and feel" issues. Those original lawsuits have since been settled. The latest versions of the two operating systems, MacOS X Yosemite and Windows 7, 8, and the soon to be released version 10, have more key user interface similarities than differences.

In some respects, for current users, it is more a matter of personal preference over the details. Some users like the organizational principle of a "Start" button in Windows. Others prefer the overall aesthetic of the Mac experience, claiming that many shared features (like the multitouch gesture responsiveness of the touchpad) just work better on a Mac.

There is a bigger difference in user interface features between desktop operating systems and mobile device operating systems. Mobile device user interfaces with a touchscreen emphasize simplicity and ease of use. This makes mobile device user interfaces more suited for simple tasks, while desktop user interfaces relying on mice and keyboards are better suited for complex tasks. The Windows 8 operating system presents users with an interesting option (that some love and some hate), because it attempts to merge elements of a mobile touchscreen interface with a traditional desktop interface.

A computing platform's user interface approach has an influence on individual tools. For example, a film school student may need to do a lot of video editing. A video-editing app like iMovie is available for the iPad tablet device platform. However, the desktop computer version of iMovie for editing video has a better user interface. It is much easier to use iMovie with a combination of mouse and keyboard input on a desktop computer than with a tablet computer's touchscreen interface.

So when selecting a computing platform, users must consider whether the individual tools for a particular platform provide an appropriate user interface for the key tasks the user wants to perform. The platform itself will impose some constraints, like touchscreen versus mouse and keyboard. The individual apps themselves will offer different user interface options and constraints as well.

All modern computing platforms provide some form of *network connectivity* allowing any device to provide access to the Internet. However, the speed and range of the connection can vary from platform to platform. For example, maximum portability is provided by a tablet with Wi-Fi and cellular antennas, which will allow users to search for things on the web from almost anywhere. Being in a building with local wireless network is not necessary. On the other hand, maximum bandwidth for high-quality video conferencing is more likely to be provided by a desktop or laptop computer with a wired Ethernet connection to a fast school network.

Operating systems are an important computing platform dimension that can have a wide-ranging effect on what services and features are available to users. For example, some users favor platforms using the Windows operating system because a lot of business-related software is available only for Windows. On the other hand, those working in video and graphic arts often favor the MacOS X operating system because many of the best artistic tools are available only for MacOS X.

Different operating systems also provide competing software and data "ecosystems." For example, personal and work data for users owning multiple devices are shared seamlessly between Apple devices using MacOS X on desktop and laptop computers and iOS on mobile devices. Only Apple's computing platforms enjoy the high levels of easy data access provided by Apple's software and data ecosystem. Other companies like Google and Microsoft offer competing software and data ecosystem options for Windows and Android operating system users.

Some data are optimized for one particular company's ecosystem, but can still be shared between platforms. Email and calendar data are two examples. Microsoft Windows, MacOS X, Android, Chrome, and other operating system platforms are able to access email and calendar data from a variety of sources. However, preferred access features still exist within one company's family of products. For example, Microsoft's Outlook email program still provides the best connectivity to Microsoft's Exchange email and calendar services software.

Peripheral device availability and compatibility also need to be considered to some extent when selecting appropriate computing platforms. Most common peripherals like printers, scanners, and projectors are compatible with all the major computing platforms. However, some newer technologies don't have the broad cross-platform compatibility built in yet. For example, wireless video devices like Apple TV and Chromecast, have platform hardware and software limitations. Apple TV works only with iOS and MacOS X devices. Chromecast will work with Android, iOS, Mac, and Windows devices, but only with "Google Cast Ready Apps."

More broadly speaking, a computing platform's ability to work with a school's existing technology infrastructure is important. Most common services provided by a school's existing technology infrastructure like wireless network access, file sharing, and email services generally work with any computing platform. However, specialized services related to testing, grades, personal data, and even printing, may be platform specific.

Cost

The cost of purchasing and operating computing devices is another important factor to consider when trying to select a computing platform. There are several cost related subareas to consider:

- Cost of initial purchase
  - Computing devices
  - Software
  - Peripherals
- Cost of ownership
  - Maintenance
  - Replacement cycle

The cost of initially purchasing the equipment is often the biggest cost involved in the selection of a computing platform. Not only must the main computing devices be purchased, but the appropriate software and peripherals must be purchased as well. For a large number of devices, the cost of software licenses for each device can often be expensive. Some computing platforms have the advantage of being bundled with a lot of included essential software. For example, some computers are sold with productivity or entertainment software preloaded. Other platforms boast the use of free online apps and services, making most software purchases unnecessary. This can lower the initial cost of purchase substantially.

The cost of ownership is often not considered as carefully as it should be. Any computing platform will require some regular maintenance of both the software and hardware. For example, on the software side, many antivirus programs require a yearly subscription, adding to the cost of ownership.

On the hardware side, some laptops have batteries that need to be replaced every year or two because of the batteries' short service life, Furthermore, depending on the hardware build quality and software support provided, the useful service life of a computing device can vary widely. Some computing platforms require complete replacement of devices every three years, while other platforms can last five or more years. Trade magazines and organizations like CNET.com, PCMag.com, and MacWorld.com offer regular reviews and comparisons of current products to help estimate the cost of ownership.

The cost of purchasing and owning computing devices from various platforms varies widely. Bigger and faster does not always mean more expensive. Desktop computer prices can range from as low as a couple hundred dollars to several thousands of dollars. Similarly, laptop computer prices can range from as low as a couple hundred dollars to several thousands of dollars. Mobile computing devices can range from as low as a couple hundred dollars to almost a thousand dollars. Once again, using resources from online trade organizations can help with performance and cost estimates.

DESKTOPS, LAPTOPS, AND TABLETS

Computing platforms currently available span the full gamut of (1) physical functionality, (2) computational functionality, and (3) cost combinations. For example, there are large inexpensive desktop computers with lots of computing power, tiny expensive mobile devices with limited computational functionality, as well as large moderately priced mobile devices with lots of computational functionality.

To help structure the discussion of the various platform strengths and weaknesses, three broad device categories on the physical form spectrum will be considered in order: (1) desktops, (2) laptops, and (3) tablets. These three tend to provide the most computational functionality for tasks that may be performed in a school setting. The strengths and weakness of these three are also discussed as they relate to performing common schools tasks such as:

1. Conducting web research
2. Communicating with email and social media
3. Writing and printing papers
4. Creating and sharing presentations
5. Facilitating interactive classroom activities
6. Facilitating activities outside of a dedicated computer lab
7. Working with graphics and multimedia

Desktops

Computing devices in the desktop computer category tend to be the largest in physical size and weight. They are available in a wide variety of styles and options that attempt to balance convenience, computational power, and cost. All desktop computers usually have (1) a box or tower case that houses the main computer processor, memory, storage, and built-in peripherals; (2) a keyboard and mouse for user input; and (3) a monitor for displaying text and graphics.

A variation on the standard desktop is an "all-in-one" computer that integrates the computer case with the display. An all-in-one computer reduces the amount of desk space required, but then also reduces the upgradability of the computer. All-in-one styles are available for both Windows and Macintosh operating system platforms (see figure 5.3).

All-in-one computers also tend to be a little more expensive. With computers, providing a device in a smaller package generally costs more because it is more difficult to manufacture. So smaller desktop computers with the same computational power as larger desktops tend to cost more.

Figure 5.3. Examples of Windows and Macintosh all-in-one computers.

Computer components like hard drives also share this inverse relationship. If two components have the same features, the component with the smaller physically size will tend to cost more.

As far as computational functionality is concerned, desktop systems will tend to provide the most processing power, the largest software options, and the most flexible and varied interface and peripheral options. Most desktops used in schools will typically run either the Windows operating system or the MacOS X operating system. Linux is also available for desktops, but tends to be less popular because of the smaller library of apps and lower levels of technical support available.

From a cost point of view, a very wide range of prices is available for desktop computers. Low-end desktops are available for a couple hundred dollars while professional-level performance desktop computers cost several thousands of dollars. Desktops providing a reasonable mix of performance for price are widely available and are typically priced between $500 and $900.

Software for desktop computers tends to be expensive. Common software tools for word processing and presentations typically cost on the order of about $200 for a suite of tools like Microsoft Office. Licenses for advanced multimedia tools and educational software can exceed thousands of dollars for a multiyear classroom set of licenses. While vendors do typically offer lower "education" pricing for their products, the cost of software can still be very high.

The cost of ownership of a set of desktop computers is not excessive compared with other platform categories. Because desktops aren't usually moved around a lot, they tend to not suffer damage from dropping or rough handling. Also, desktop computer components like memory and even central processing units can be upgraded to extend the life of a desktop system.

Desktops are able to support most common schools tasks with sufficient power and user convenience. As shown in table 5.1, most common tasks are well suited for a desktop computer. The facilitation of outside-of-classroom activities and some classroom activities are two exceptions, however, because desktops tend to be bulky and are not suited for activities requiring some mobility.

In summary, for tasks that require large screen sizes, easy user input, and fast processing, desktops are probably the best choice. They provide the most upgradability and computational functionality of any platform. They also tend to provide the best value in terms of computational functionality for the price. As long as the task does not require moving the computing device around a lot, desktop computers can meet many school activity needs at a reasonable price. They tend to have a long service life

Table 5.1. Common School Tasks of Desktops

School Task	*Computational Power and Functionality*
Conducting web research	Meets
Communicating with email and social media	Meets
Writing and printing papers	Meets
Creating and sharing presentations	Meets
Facilitating interactive classroom activities	Varies
Facilitating activities outside of a dedicated computer lab	Does Not Meet
Working with graphics and multimedia	Meets

and provide a large library of high-quality software tools and peripheral devices for students and teachers to use.

LAPTOPS

Computing devices in the laptop computer category are small and light enough to be portable. As the name implies, laptops are small enough to be used on a person's lap, and offer users with screen sizes and computing power levels comparable to desktop computers. However, this smaller size makes laptops generally more expensive than desktops offering similar computational features.

Laptop computers have a foldable body with a display screen on the top half and a keyboard and touchpad on the bottom half. Most processor, memory, and power components are usually housed in the body underneath the keyboard. This makes laptops more difficult to upgrade, but some laptops do allow users to have relatively easy access to replace common internal components like the hard drive or RAM.

With the limited internal space, external peripheral devices must be relied on to expand the features of a laptop. Access to more storage, alternate input devices, larger display screens, and other services can be provided through a laptop's peripheral ports. USB, FireWire, and Thunderbolt are among the most popular peripheral interfaces available on laptops.

Laptops are also available in a wide variety of styles and options that attempt to balance convenience, computational power, and cost. Larger laptops usually have built-in optical drives for reading and writing DVD media, and they usually have a high-capacity internal hard drive. Smaller laptops often do not include an optical drive and sometimes use a solid-state drive (SSD) for primary storage to reduce size and weight. SSDs tend to be faster than hard drives as well, but are also much more expensive.

Higher-end laptops offer computational speeds that rival some of the fastest desktops. Many use aluminum external bodies for extra durability. A class of laptops designed to maximize portability called *ultrabooks* offer very low weight and body thicknesses that are comparable to tablet computers.

Laptops use the same operating systems as desktops, and so generally have access to all the same software and peripheral tools available to desktops. The software cost issues and performance issues of desktop computers are also shared by most laptop computers. Every laptop needs its own full license of any software tools installed on it.

The exception to this is "netbooks," which do not run Windows or MacOS X operating systems, and technically do not require the purchasing of separate software for standard office and web research tasks. Netbooks are a low-cost option providing the convenient laptop form factor with a reduced feature set (including less internal memory and slower processors). An example of a netbook is Chromebook built by Samsung running Google's Chrome OS operating system.

Netbooks are not portable versions of desktop computers like other fully featured laptops. Netbooks make use of cloud-based applications where the software technically runs on online service company servers, and the netbooks primarily function as display and user-input devices. Chromebooks offer word processing services this way by allowing users to run Google Docs through the Chromebook's web browser. Other web-based application services including photo editing and video playback services can also be used through netbooks.

However, this dependence on online services has some key limitations. First, netbooks need to be connected to a wireless network continuously to function properly. Second, a slow network will make the use of all applications slower. Also, with the aim toward lower costs, some netbooks seem to have lower build quality than regular laptops, with studies pointing to a lower general durability for netbooks (e.g., Linder, 2009).

Fully featured laptops are able to support most common schools tasks with sufficient power and user convenience. As shown in table 5.2, most common tasks are well suited for a laptop computer. Laptops can be more useful than desktops for tasks that require activities outside of a computer lab. They have batteries and are convenient enough to use when moving to different classroom and school settings.

There are some limitations posed by the battery life of laptops. Activities that require use for longer than two to three hours may be problematic for older laptops. Many newer laptops boast batteries that can be used for more than six hours, with some able to provide enough power for more than fourteen hours of use (Krawczyk, 2014).

Table 5.2. Common School Tasks of Laptops

School Task	*Computational Power and Functionality*
Conducting web research	Meets
Communicating with email and social media	Meets
Writing and printing papers	Meets
Creating and sharing presentations	Meets
Facilitating interactive classroom activities	Varies
Facilitating activities outside of a dedicated computer lab	Meets
Working with graphics and multimedia	Can Meet

Netbooks are able to support many common schools tasks with sufficient power and user convenience, but not tasks requiring a lot of computational power and speed. As shown in table 5.3, some common tasks are well suited for a netbook, but not all. Netbooks require constant wireless connectivity to be fully useful. Activities in computer labs and outside of computer labs will only be supported as long as a wireless signal is available in those settings. Netbooks do not have sufficient computing power for reliable graphics and multimedia work.

In summary, fully featured laptops can be seen as portable versions of desktops. With the exception of the most processor-intensive and peripheral-intensive tasks, they can do almost anything desktops can do. Their portability allows their computing power to be used in settings outside of a computer lab even when no electrical outlets are available. Their smaller size, however, leads to a much higher price per unit than a comparable desktop computer. They tend to have a shorter service life because of the increased wear and tear experienced by portable devices.

Table 5.3. Common School Tasks of Netbooks

School Task	*Computational Power and Functionality*
Conducting web research	Meets
Communicating with email and social media	Meets
Writing and printing papers	Meets
Creating and sharing presentations	Meets
Facilitating interactive classroom activities	Varies
Facilitating activities outside of a dedicated computer lab	Varies
Working with graphics and multimedia	Does Not Meet

Netbooks share the portability advantages of full-featured laptops, but provide less computational functionality. They cost much less, however, and so may be suitable for many situations. As long as processor-intensive tasks (like graphics or video work) are not required and reliable wireless network coverage is available, netbooks can be very capable tools.

Tablets

Computing devices in the tablet computer category are even smaller and lighter than laptops. They can be held like clipboards, and offer touch-screen interfaces for ease of use and simplicity. Their screen sizes are smaller than those of most laptops and desktops, and their computing power levels are typically much lower than laptops and desktops.

Tablets are generally less expensive per unit than laptops, but they provide less computational value for the price. The least expensive tablets cost about $200 and may have a limited suite of software tools available. Higher end tablets with lots of built-in memory can cost almost a thousand dollars, but offer much less computational functionality than a similarly priced desktop or laptop.

The tablet platform's extremely portable size and weight make them usable in situations where using even the smallest laptops would not be convenient. Tablets can be held in one hand and provided with input through the touch-screen interface using the other hand. By comparison, laptops must be put down on a table or lap to comfortably enter input using the keyboard or touchpad.

All tablets are equipped for wireless networking using Wi-Fi. Some tablet models are equipped with cellular antennas to enable Internet access from almost anywhere. Available ports vary from tablet to tablet, with many Android operating system–based tablets like the Samsung Galaxy providing USB ports. By comparison, iOS operating system–based tablets like the Apple iPad Air have a proprietary port for power and data transfer needs, and require separate adapters to connect to USB devices.

Tablets are also available in a wide variety of styles and options that attempt to balance convenience, computational power, and cost. Higher-end tablets offer higher computational speeds, larger built-in memory chips, and larger and brighter screens that result in a smoother user experience with better graphics and video performance. Lower-end tablets are slower and smaller, but can cost significantly less.

Tablets are dominated by two main operating systems: Android and iOS. Android is an open-source operating system for mobile devices and is currently the most widely used mobile operating system for smartphones and tablets (Mahapatra, 2013). iOS is a mobile device operating system developed by Apple and is used exclusively by Apple hardware, including the iPad family of tablet devices and iPhone family of smartphones. Other companies also offer competing mobile operating systems (Microsoft has a mobile version of Windows for example), but Android and iOS are by far the most widely used.

iOS is considered to be the most popular and polished operating system for tablets. It has the largest software ecosystem and appears to provide the cleanest user experience (Colbert, 2013). Android is the next most popular operating system for tablets. It is less polished but preferred by some people for its larger feature set and customization options. Tablets using both of these operating systems can perform the same basic tasks for school-related situations, with one sometimes doing the task a little bit better than the other.

Tablets are able to support many common school tasks, but some tasks cannot be completed as easily as they would with a desktop or laptop (see table 5.4). For example, tasks that require a lot of typing are difficult on a tablet. Using an external keyboard can help, but that makes the tablet less mobile. Tasks that require a lot of memory or processing power, like high-quality graphics and video work, are not suited for tablets either.

For tasks that require mobility, tablets shine because they usually have batteries that can last eight to ten hours, and with no internal moving parts, they tend to be quite durable. If ease of use is important, tablets are also a good choice because of the simple and intuitive interface provided by tablet touch screens and their operating systems. However, from a purely functional point of view, tablets are not as useful as laptops because they cannot address as many tasks well.

In summary, tablets are a great computing platform for tasks where mobility is of the highest importance. With a long battery life, durable build, and intuitive touch interface, tasks like taking notes during a school trip, taking quick pictures and movies, and viewing relevant documents and media are well suited for a tablet computer. They provide much less

Table 5.4. Common School Tasks of Tablets

School Task	*Computational Power and Functionality*
Conducting web research	Meets
Communicating with email and social media	Meets
Writing and printing papers	Can Meet with Peripherals
Creating and sharing presentations	Can Meet with Peripherals
Facilitating interactive classroom activities	Varies
Facilitating activities outside of a dedicated computer lab	Meets
Working with graphics and multimedia	Does Not Meet

computational functionality and cost a lot in light of their computational limitations. However, the convenience provided by the small physical form can often make them worth the extra cost.

SUMMARY

Computing platforms come in many shapes and sizes. A computing platform generally means some computing hardware running some operating system software. A desktop computer from Dell running the Windows 8 operating system is an example of a computing platform. A MacBook Pro laptop running the MacOS X operating system is an example of a computing platform. A Samsung tablet computer running the Android operating system is an example of a computing platform.

When comparing computing platform options, the factors that should be considered can be placed into three main categories: physical functionality, computational functionality, and cost. Physical functionality includes common physical properties like device size, weight, and build quality. Computational functionality includes properties like processing speed, network connectivity, and software tool availability. Cost issues include both the cost of initial purchase and the cost of long term ownership.

Desktop computers typically provide the best value in terms of processing power and longevity for a given price. They are usually larger than other platforms and are not good for moving around. But they can be upgraded easily and are not costly to maintain relative to other platforms.

Tablet computers are on the other end of the spectrum, providing the least value in terms of processing power. However, they provide maximum portability and offer a touch-screen interface that is simple and intuitive to use. The physical flexibility and software simplicity of tablets often makes tablets fun to use for quick activities in all sorts of school settings.

When the broadest level of usability is sought, laptop computers may be the best option because of their combination of computational functionality and physical portability. They can perform virtually all of the functions performed by desktop computers, but at a higher cost per unit. Within the laptop family there is also a range of options from the least expensive netbooks to the most expensive ultrabooks.

The choice of computing platform for a school laboratory or department should be determined by the desired functionality of that laboratory or department. Depending on how the computers plan to be used, any one of the three major physical form factors (desktops, laptops, and tablets) could be the best candidate. A careful analysis of the needs of students and teachers will help a school purchase the right computing platform for their school.

CASE STUDY

You are an assistant principal with some technical proficiency. The principal often relies on your advice for technology decisions. Currently, two departments in your school would like new computers to be purchased.

The language arts department would like to purchase a classroom set of computers that will allow students to access web resources anywhere on the school grounds and view copies of short stories that they can mark up on their devices during class discussions. They would also like to be able to have students type up papers in class with their computing devices and print their papers. A one-to-one student-to-computer ratio is desired.

The science department would also like to purchase a classroom set of computers that will enable students to "practice science" anywhere, not just in a science lab. They would like students to be able to make measurements outside, and log them on their devices. They would like students to be able to write observation notes, take quick pictures, and record short video. Back in the classroom, students should be able to type up reports and print. Additionally, they should be able to access and use online resources like physical simulations and watch videos of science phenomenon. Being able to edit the pictures and videos would be nice too. A one-to-one ratio is not required because students often work in pairs.

The principal has a budget of $40,000 and would like your recommendations. What kind of computers should the school buy for each department? What should the minimal hardware specifications be? Why do these choices make sense given the student activity needs of each department?

EXERCISES AND DISCUSSION QUESTIONS

1. What are the main computing platforms that are often used in school situations?
2. When making comparisons between different computing platforms, what dimensions should be examined? Why are these important?
3. If a long service life is desired from a computing platform in a stationary computer lab area, which platform would be most suitable? What features should be sought within this computing platform?
4. What are the main strengths and weaknesses of laptop computers? What kinds of tasks are they most suitable for? What is their biggest weakness?

5. If a school already has a set of desktop computers from a certain platform (either Mac or Windows), and this school wants to purchase a set of tablet computers, why might choosing iOS devices make the most sense? Why might choosing Android devices make the most sense? What types of benefits would be enjoyed by choosing one mobile platform over another given the existing set of desktop computers?

REFERENCES

Colbert, D. (2013). Which is the superior mobile OS: iOS, Android, or Windows 8? *TechRepublic.* Retrieved from http://www.techrepublic.com/blog/tablets-in-the-enterprise/which-is-the-superior-mobile-os-ios-android-or-windows-8/

Krawczyk, K. (2014). Which laptops have the lengthiest battery life of them all? *Digital Trends.* Retrieved from http://www.digitaltrends.com/computing/which-laptops-have-the-best-longest-battery-life/

Linder, B. (2009). Study: Netbooks fail 20% more than other laptops. *Liliputing.* Retrieved from http://liliputing.com/2009/11/study-netbooks-fail-20-more-than-other-laptops.html

Mahapatra, L. (2013). Android vs. iOS: What's the most popular mobile operating system in your country? *International Business Times.* Retrieved from http://www.ibtimes.com/android-vs-ios-whats-most-popular-mobile-operating-system-your-country-1464892

SIX

Security and Maintenance

OBJECTIVES

At the conclusion of this chapter, the reader will be able to:

1. Understand the concepts of risk assessment, assets, threats, vulnerabilities, and annualized loss expectancy (ISTE 1, 3, 4).
2. Describe physical and software security threats, countermeasures, and layered security (ISTE 3, 4, 5).
3. Describe an intrusion detection system and an intrusion prevention system (ISTE 2, 3, 4).
4. Explain the main concepts related to the hardening of operating systems, encryption, virtual private networks, firewalls, and user security policies (ISTE 2, 3, 4).
5. List the reasons for using antivirus and antimalware programs (ISTE 3, 4, 5).
6. Describe techniques for maintaining computer hardware and software (ISTE 1, 3, 4).

COMPUTER NETWORK SECURITY AND MAINTENANCE

Important information of an educational institution such as grades, student and employee personal data, financial budgets, safety and security procedures, and human resource records are often located on school district network systems. These systems, which expose vulnerability, can often be accessed via the Internet. Consequently, all confidential information stored on any computer needs to be secured and maintained properly. Only through securely maintained systems can information on computers remain confidential and reliable.

Vulnerability, Assets, and Risk Assessment

Vulnerability is defined as the degree of exposure to attacks to the data in computer systems. Control has an inverse relationship with vulnerability. The more control is implemented on an asset, the less vulnerable it becomes. As a result, security and safety can be achieved. Assets should be classified according to their values and vulnerabilities so the correct amount of security can be used to protect against attacks.

Assets consist of hardware, software, and the data stored in a networking system. A threat is defined as anything that can attack vulnerable assets. The loss of data could be a result of malicious hacking, natural disasters, terrorism, or human error. Furthermore, hacker attacks could seriously damage educational institutions' private assets. To protect against such attacks, countermeasures can be implemented to protect the computer hardware and software from harm.

To establish secure computer network systems, it is necessary to identify hardware and software that are potentially vulnerable. The identification process is referred to as *risk assessment*. *Risk* is defined as the possibility of an undesirable breach of security. Risk assessment is the method used to evaluate and manage threats in an organized manner. There are two types of risks: qualitative and quantitative.

Qualitative risk compares the asset values and rates them against each other. The vulnerability and threat values depend on the value of the asset (Sims, 2012). Through qualitative risk assessment, the information technology (IT) department can determine the degree of the risk of assets. The basic formula for qualitative risk is Risk = Asset × Vulnerability × Threat.

Quantitative risk identifies the risk taken on the assets to determine the total effects of dollar amount, exposure, and frequency. This method gives the exact amount of risk that needs to be taken for an individual asset. Exposure is a variable that depends on the use or abuse of the network. The number of times per year the asset is exposed to danger is called frequency. The basic formula for quantitative risk is calculated by the annualized loss expectancy (ALE): ALE = Asset × Exposure × Frequency.

Through risk assessment, the type of hardware and software that is used is prioritized, classified, and categorized according to the level of the vulnerability of an attack. All security measures should be implemented to reduce the possibility of any damage to the computer systems and to the data being stored. By keeping accurate records of attacks, the network administrator can determine the vulnerability levels of the attacks. These records can also help determine whether the attacks are from within or outside of the network.

Network and computer maintenance are essential for productive and continuous operations. The IT department's help desk at each school should be proactive in scheduling and implementing maintenance procedures. If preventive measures are taken by the school professionals, hardware and software problems should not occur often. Consequently, the number of last-minute problems and fixes should occur occasionally.

Virus, Malware, Adware, and Spyware

By definition, a *computer virus* is malicious code that can damage the programs on a computer by altering them. *Malware* is defined as malicious code that damages the software by accessing personal information stored on computers. *Adware, spyware, Trojan horses,* and *worms* are categories of malware. Antivirus and antimalware programs should be used to clean up the infected computers.

Adware can flood the computer with pop-ups and unwanted advertisements. Adware and spyware can sometimes be removed by uninstalling the suspected adware or spyware programs. On a Windows computers, this can be done by accessing the Windows Control Panel, clicking on "Add/Remove Programs," highlighting the unwanted programs, clicking "Remove," and then restarting the computer. On a MacOS computer, suspected programs can be dragged into the trash, and then the computer should be restarted. Adware and spyware that are difficult to find can be removed by scanning the computer with a commercially available antivirus program.

Through spyware, hackers can obtain users' contact, email, and financial information by tracking the websites visited. The following are some examples of how spyware can infiltrate a system:

- Unwanted emails that include attachments
- Unblocked cookies (running undesired sets of code that capture information) that can slow down the computer system and cause undesired advertisements and email to an account (cookies contain the visited websites' information, which needs to be cleaned on a regular basis)
- Scripts, pop-ups, and advertisements
- Unblocked Java programs

Trojan Horses and Worms

A Trojan horse is a form of malware that can hide as usable software, but its intentions are extremely harmful. For example, some security tools and screen savers may look very attractive to download, but once downloaded, their intentions are to access personal information and harm the user's computer and data. To prevent a Trojan horse from attacking a computer, it is important that the user only interacts with pop-up messages from websites that he or she knows are trustworthy.

A worm is a special kind of virus that spreads to different computers without the user having to click on an executable file or pop-up. When communicating through email or other software, the worm has the ability to clone itself onto other computers. As a result, the bandwidth of an infected network system is negatively affected. This means that the network becomes stifled and legitimate data flow decreases. If the worm is not handled through antivirus programs or other IT procedures, eventually all computer operations can stop and the system may crash.

As part of proper network maintenance procedures, the network administrator installs and maintains antivirus programs in the computers. Some antivirus and antimalware software is free. These programs can be scheduled to perform automatic updates and run on a weekly, daily, or hourly basis to protect computers. Once an antimalware program scans a computer and finds viruses and malware, the user can quarantine and delete the unwanted items. Malwarebytes Anti-malware and Super Anti-spyware are examples of good security programs that can be used to prevent viruses and malware from harming computers.

PHYSICAL SECURITY THREATS AND COUNTERMEASURES

Physical security threats to computers are caused by adverse climate conditions, natural disasters, destructive acts, and accidents. Countermeasures against physical security threats to computers can be taken by creating a secure environment. Maintaining appropriate room temperature is crucial for protecting computers from adverse weather conditions, which can cause malfunctioning of the equipment. Implementing emergency preparation procedures and using regulated power supplies are considered countermeasures. Examples of other actions that can be taken to create a secure school environment include:

- Building facilities that meet the safety and electrical codes
- Installing equipment such as alarm systems, fire extinguishers, retinal scanners, key locks, surge protectors, video cameras, and voice analyzers
- Employing security guards to keep buildings safe and secure
- Constructing rooms with high ceilings and fire-proof walls
- Placing high-security locks on the doors of the computer rooms
- Installing security film and security screens on locked windows

- Placing signs in computer rooms reading "No drinking, eating, or smoking."
- Keeping the temperature between 45 and 70 degrees Fahrenheit in rooms with computer equipment
- Keeping the humidity between 30% and 70% in rooms with computer equipment
- Using uninterrupted power supplies, which help protect devices during power failures
- Taking precautions against static electricity by installing antistatic carpets and floors
- Using outlets wisely by not overloading circuits with too many devices

Further countermeasures against computer and network security can be taken by implementing the following steps:

- Install computers, equipment, and cables properly. For example, do not install computers near doors, heaters, and air conditioners.
- Repair and maintain computers, cables, and equipment such as scanners, printers, video, and fax machines.
- Keep confidential information in places where access is limited.
- Make it hard to steal the equipment. Use security cables, special keys and screws that cannot be compromised in order to physically connect equipment to furniture.
- Allow limited access to computers with sensitive information and monitor all school personnel use of these computers.
- Store laptop computers in locked locations.
- Require individual user identification and password to access computers and devices such as printers, copiers, scanners, and fax machines.
- Shred confidential papers and wet them with water before disposing of them in common dumpsters.

SOFTWARE SECURITY THREATS AND COUNTERMEASURES

Applying software security controls to protect computers, networks, and data from threats is called *layered security, layered defense,* or *countermeasures.* Layered security is similar to securing a school building. Using two or three door locks for a school building entrance is a more secure system than an entrance with one door lock. Each locked door represents a software security layer. The more locked doors, the more secure the building. In a similar way, the more software defense layers in a computer system, the more secure the network.

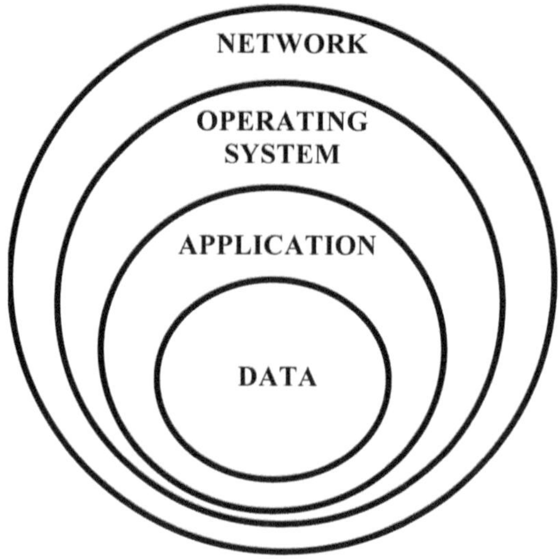

Figure 6.1. A diagram of layered security.

There are different layers of defense to protect against any threats and attacks. To block attacks, each layer is vulnerable to certain types of breaches. The data layer is the core or center of layered security and it is within the application layer. The application layer is surrounded by the operating system (OS) layer. The OS layer is within the network layer. Figure 6.1 presents the diagram of layered security.

Layered Security

Layered security or layered defense blocks threats against networks, computers, and data. With the use of layered security, each layer protects the data at the core. The network layer is the outer layer and it is most at risk without a firewall. A firewall is the first defense mechanism to protect network computers from any outside attacks. It is a defense device that separates the network into two parts: protected and unprotected. A firewall is the layer of protection between the Internet and the network (see the subsection "Firewall" for more in-depth information). Firewalls can be implemented on specialized devices or as software running on a router.

Blocking unauthorized users from gaining access to the system is called *denial of service* (DoS). It uses two types of software: intrusion detection system (IDS) and intrusion prevention system (IPS). IDS detects when an unauthorized user attempts to access the computers and the information within the network. The IDS also informs the IT department about potential threats. For example, Snort is an open-source IDS software program that performs real-time network and computer traffic analysis. IDS also logs information about malicious activity by using three detection methods:

1. Signature-based intrusion detection—Monitors traffic for matching signatures. When a match is found, the IDS takes action to block any unauthorized activity.
2. Statistical anomaly-based intrusion detection—Based on average traffic conditions. If there is any activity outside of the average, then IDS takes action to block the attack.
3. Stateful protocol analysis intrusion detection—Identifies deviations of protocols by observing activity against general guidelines before blocking the threat.

Any kind of software and hardware bugs or issues can be fixed after analyzing the network to minimize threats. An IPS is a built-in network system that monitors traffic. The IPS detects an attack and blocks future attempts from the same sources. Through web usage analysis, it detects any intruder traffic that could harm the system.

Hardening of the OS is a way to implement security at the OS level (see subsection of this chapter titled "Hardening of the Operating Systems" for more in-depth information). To harden and defend the OS, it is important to install security software patches. Patches and updates are offered by different OSs that the device uses and are easily downloaded. Examples include Windows security updates, Microsoft baseline security analyzer, and the open source Nessus.

A proxy server provides an additional line of defense for hardening the OS. A proxy server prevents access to undesirable sites, downloads, and scanning of information. It blocks the known websites that attack the networks. The proxy server also serves as a back up to ensure that corrupt websites cannot be accessed.

The central layer, which is the data layer, offers the best defense because it is protected and surrounded by multiple security layers. A breach in all of the other layers must take place for the data layer to be affected. The data layer needs to be protected to prevent sharing of confidential information, as well as preventing viruses from corrupting the data. There are viruses that can also remain undetected within the data layer until they are activated.

Virtual Private Network

Encryption is the conversion of data to a format that can only be understood by the transmitter and the receiver. The transmitter encrypts the data before it sends the encrypted data to the receiver. The receiver then decrypts the data. Smart encryption codes are necessary so that no one else, besides the receiver, is able to break the code and decipher the data. Through the implementation of encryption, data privacy, protection, and security are achieved.

A virtual private network (VPN) is the secure connection between the school employees' computers and the school's private network through the Internet. Security is achieved by the encryption of data. When intruders try to decrypt the code, the VPN blocks their attempts. An authorized user initiates the VPN connection, the company server authenticates the data and connectivity is established. The advantages of implementing VPNs are:

- Computer and network security is established because only the authorized users can access the network.
- Multiple geographic locations can benefit from VPN connections.
- Employees at remote locations can access the company's intranet where local software resources are available for employee use.
- Employees at remote distances can connect to the VPN reliably and with minimal down times.
- Schools save time and money because employees can perform work from any location without having to travel to their schools.

VPNs use three different protocols: point-to-point tunneling protocol (PPTP), layer 2 tunneling protocol (L2TP), and Internet protocol security (IPSec). In PPTP, a whole data packet is added within the main information packet. This added data packet is called an *encapsulation*. This process occurs when information goes through Internet protocol (IP). The encapsulation process ensures protection of the contents from public and transmitting of data through the tunnel (Tyson & Crawford, 2011). The transmitting or receiving computer encodes and decodes the data packets into larger units of information called *frames*.

Tunneling refers to transmitting and receiving data with encryptions. For the PPTP, authentication is achieved through extensible authentication protocol (EAP) and challenge-handshake authentication protocol (CHAP). EAP is the protocol implemented when Internet access is needed through a wireless computer or laptop. EAP works with authentication tools such as passwords and encryptions.

To access the Internet through a wireless connection using the EAP, the transmitting computer requests a connection with the receiving computer through a wireless access point (WAP). The server, which is connected to the WAP, asks for transmitting computer's password and identification to authenticate the connection. The transmitter sends the password informa-

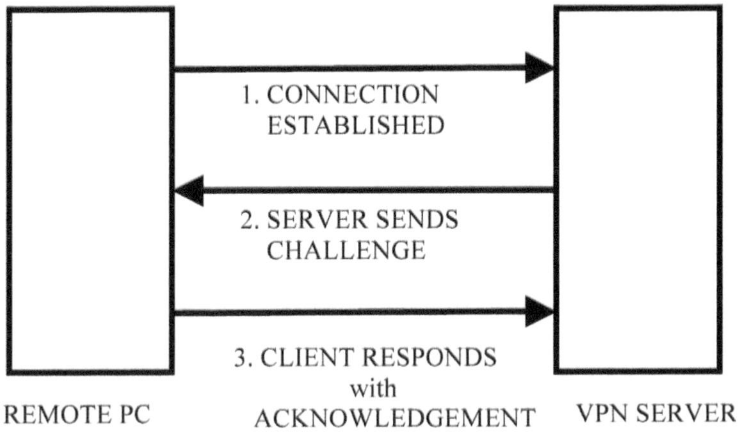

Figure 6.2. Three-way handshaking for VPN.

tion to the server. Once the server secures authentication then the connection is established and the transmitting computer sends the information through the Internet.

The CHAP uses three-way handshaking for the authentication process, which is initiated by a remote computer. The remote computer first establishes a connection with the VPN server. Then the server sends a request, called a *challenge,* to the remote computer. Through the challenge, the server allows the data to be transmitted. The remote computer, in turn, responds with an acknowledgement and then data are transmitted. Figure 6.2 illustrates three-way handshaking for VPN.

L2TP is a better method than PPTP. It uses EAP, CHAP, and other authentication methods such as password authentication protocol (PAP). Through PAP, a username and a password are sent from the client to the VPN server. The VPN server recognizes the username and the password to authorize transmission of the requested information.

IPSec uses two encryption methods: transport mode and tunnel mode. Transport mode encrypts data but not the source and destination addresses (headers). Tunnel mode encrypts data as well as the headers. As a result, tunnel mode is more secure but slower than transport mode.

Firewall

Firewall can be classified as follows: host-based, router-based, and screened-host firewalls. A host-based firewall is software-based and runs directly on a particular computer protecting the device against attack from the network by controlling traffic. Router-based firewall routers check inbound packets against filtering criteria to determine whether to accept or reject the packets.

Screened-host firewalls use router packet rules to allow traffic only between the Internet and public web server. This type of firewall utilizes the combination of host-based and router-based firewalls. Each screened-host firewall router separates a small network segment from other networks. If a security attack occurs it will be handled by one of the screened-host routers and the rest of the small networks will not be affected.

A firewall can be set to block unwanted advertisements that cause constant interruptions. It also slows down network systems. Using high security settings and limiting the use of unsecured Internet sites are ways to implement firewalls. A firewall uses traffic filtering through application of rules. There are three types of rules to apply for the traffic filtering of firewalls: packet filtering, circuit-level gateway, and application gateway.

During packet filtering, also known as *static filtering,* data packets are filtered according to their protocols. Protocols are rules and policies for destination IP addresses and ports and source IP addresses and ports. Packet filtering does not provide foolproof security. The format for packet filtering for VPN is shown in figure 6.3.

Packet filtering does not prevent spoofing. Spoofing makes false information appear to be correct. Through spoofing it is possible to receive wrong information. To minimize the effects of spoofing, packet filtering is used. To minimize the threat of spoofing, techniques such as circuit level gateway and application gateway are typically implemented.

A *circuit-level gateway* makes a virtual connection between the receiving computer and the proxy server. It determines if the connection between transmitting computer and the receiving computer is valid according to the configuration rules. Because the source address is validated as a function of the protocol, spoofing is much more difficult than packet filtering. The disadvantage is that circuit-level gateway requires a lot of programming. The application gateway has its own protocols that allow traffic to flow. For example, it limits file access to the server for authenticated users only. This is the most secure type of firewall. The disadvantage is that it can be very complex to set up.

ACK	SOURCE IP ADDRESS & PORT	DESTINATION IP ADDRESS & PORT	PROTOCOL	DATA	ERROR CHECKING

Figure 6.3. Format for packet filtering for VPN.

For small offices, using any kind of firewall is generally sufficient. The risk of attack is low. Windows firewall and packet filtering are suitable for small offices. In larger offices more network ports (that is, "communication channels") need to be opened to accommodate more firewall services. For example, voice over Internet protocol (VoIP) and NetMeeting both require more than twenty-five firewall services and open ports.

To set up firewalls properly, the IT department needs to implement hardware and software using the following order:

1. Install servers.
2. Load all the software.
3. Run services such as email and VoIP.
4. Set up the firewall.

There are a multitude of firewalls on the market place. Selecting the appropriate firewall depends on the software and hardware requirements. The following are some of the factors to be considered in firewall selection:

- Cost and level of protection
- The level of security needed in a specific area
- Application of security policies
- Protection and the reputation of the school
- Future cost of firewall software updates

Application of User Security Policies

User security policies are necessary to implement for the safety and security of the personal computers, laptops, and networks. User policies cover rules about password selection, Internet use, email attachments, software installation and removal, instant messaging, desktop configuration, and system administration. Password selection is one of the most important and easiest security measures that a user can implement.

To create a secure password, a user should:

- Use at least eight to twenty-one alphanumeric characters including upper and lower case letters, numbers, and special characters.
- Avoid the obvious passwords like Jack#@computer2 or Jack#1234.
- Use invisible characters that are not accessible to anyone.
- Keep passwords private.

As soon as a password is compromised, it should be changed to a new password that does not resemble the old password. For example, a password such as Computer#2@Jack is not a good alternative to Jack#@ computer2. Also, the IT department needs to be informed immediately to ensure that the data have not been compromised. For example, a compromised password can attract unwanted emails. Because emails can spread viruses easily, opening unrecognized email attachments can be damaging to the computers and networks. For the security and safety of computers, open email attachments only if they are expected or if they come from known reliable sources.

The IT department needs to approve any new software that needs to be on a school computer. The IT department also needs to ensure that the new software requirements are compatible with the OS of the computers. The new programs should meet requirements such as memory size and central processing unit speed. New software installation without the IT department's approval can cause damage to computers and networks from virus, adware, or spyware attacks.

The IT department needs to check the contents of computer hard drives to make sure that there are no security hazards. Since harmful executable (.exe) files can exist, checking all the file extensions is important for security. Through the executable files, computers install software automatically. Unless the user installs software from reliable sources, executable files can be harmful to computers.

System administration policies should be followed by new employees and by those leaving the school. New employees should be given rights to access only the functions they need. For employees leaving a school, all login accounts should be disabled. All room keys need to be returned and their computers and laptop hard drives should be cleaned. The IT department should block former employees' computer user credentials.

Hardening of the Operating System

Vulnerabilities to software attacks on computers always exist. To counter these software attacks, developers schedule OS patches. These patches and updates are necessary to protect a computer.

On a Windows platform computer, in order to apply the OS patches, browser settings need to be secured through privacy settings such as:

- Allow session cookies.
- Block the third-party cookies.
- Prompt the first-party cookies.
- Change the security settings by selecting custom settings.

Windows registry is a database that stores information about hardware, software, users, and user preferences. Modifying the default Windows registry settings makes the computer and network systems secure. To view the windows registry, the user clicks on Start > Run and types *regedit*. The user then observes the Windows registry dialog box and modifies registry settings.

Modifying the registry settings for security requires "Restricting null session access." If this setting is left on default, the network can accept any user, who can invite an outside attack. The user needs to change the setting from "Anonymous connection to any server" to "Restrict null access" and enter a setting value of one. A value of one restricts the access of unauthenticated users.

Remote access to registry settings should be limited to school administrators. They can control the security level of the passwords to access the network. The setting called "KeepAlive" sets the length of time that keeps the connection active. The "SynAttackProtect" setting protects the servers and computers from synchronize (SYN) attacks. The SYN attacks are a category of DoS attacks that flood the computers with unwanted information (Easttom, 2013). Unwanted information can slow down and overload the computers as well as the whole network.

Hardening the OS also requires shutting down computer services that are not needed. The vulnerability to hacker attacks is higher when more services are in use. On a Windows computer, to turn off a service, the user needs to click Start > Control Panel > Administrative Tools > Services. Through the dialog box the user can disable any services that are not required.

PHYSICAL AND SOFTWARE MAINTENANCE

Protecting computers and networks from harm and keeping them secure requires physical and software maintenance. Keeping computers clean and in working order is a basic and important physical maintenance action. Software maintenance includes installing and running antivirus and antimalware programs, which can help remove malicious software and create a more secure environment for computers. Backing up hard drives is also an essential part of software maintenance.

Physical Maintenance

Even though an optical mouse does not generally require any cleaning, it is important to check and dust the top of the red laser light emitter. A mechanical mouse, with a tracking ball, can collect a lot of dirt and dust. A good procedure is to disconnect the mouse, remove the tracking ball, and then clean the ball and the inside of the mouse with a nonabrasive cloth. All these procedures can be used for both wired and wireless mice.

Cleaning the monitor screen can be best accomplished by using a nonabrasive soft cloth with streak-free screen cleaning solution. A solution that contains deionized water and polymers works well. It is important to wipe gently without pressure when cleaning touch screens. Because the dust collects over time and it is damaging to the computer, it is imperative to clean the computer case, along with inside the computer. An antistatic cloth can be used to clean exterior computer surfaces. Compressed air can be used to blow out dust from areas of the computer that cannot be reached, especially around the cooling fan. Sometimes a vacuum cleaner can help remove the dust as well.

Software Maintenance

Software maintenance includes applying regular updates, using firewall protection, using hard drive memory management, and recording troubleshooting event logs. Computers or laptops may cease to operate because of virus or malware attacks. Therefore, backing up data stored on computers frequently is necessary. When computer hardware or software problems occur, the backed-up information can be used.

Running a disk cleanup program is another way of maintaining computers. On a Windows computer, this program can be found in the Control Panel. Figure 6.4 shows a screen shot outlining the steps disk cleanup

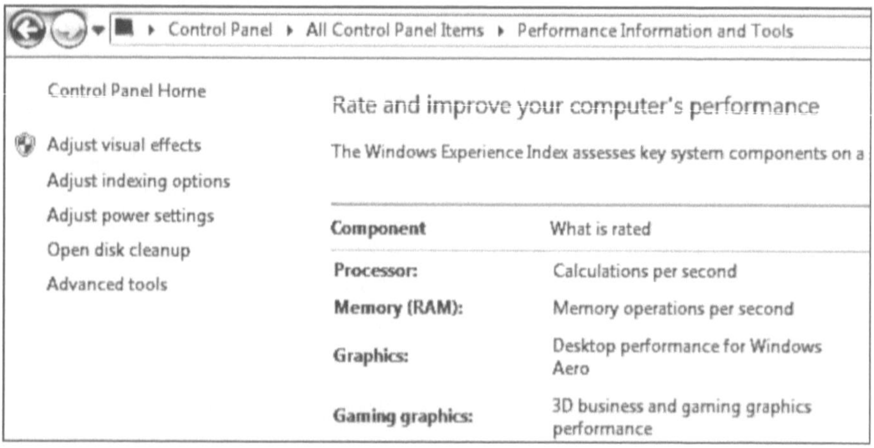

Figure 6.4. A screen shot outlining the steps to open disk cleanup.

follows. After the cleaning of temporary and unnecessary files, more usable storage space becomes available. More available storage space can enable a computer to run faster.

Another way to create storage space is backing up data. Backing up data on computers can be accomplished through the use of external hard drives. Emailing the important files to the user and deleting them from a computer also increases memory space. Saving files on a cloud server using services such as Dropbox or Google Drive can also free up storage space.

SUMMARY

All confidential information stored on computers should be classified according to values and vulnerabilities. Vulnerability needs to be calculated to protect assets such as hardware, software, and the data stored in a networking system. Vulnerability is the level of threat to which the computer systems are exposed. Managing threats through risk assessment can be calculated through quantitative and qualitative methods. All security measures should be implemented to reduce the possibility of any damage to the computer systems and to the data being stored.

To create a secure and safe environment, countermeasures can be taken against physical security threats to computers. Layered security or layered defense blocks threats against networks, computers, and data. With the use of layered security, each layer protects the data at the core.

An IDS, hardening of the OS, VPN, and firewall are used to increase security. An IDS detects and blocks unauthorized users and notifies the IT department about an intrusion attack. Hardening of the OS is the process of installing patches and updates to the OS to protect the data and software. VPN services limit access to the computer network according to the security clearance level of the user.

A firewall is the first layer of defense against network attacks. A firewall filters the traffic according to protocols set by the IT department to allow data to arrive from reliable sources only. There are three types of rules to apply for the traffic filtering of firewalls: packet filtering, circuit-level gateway, and application gateway.

User security policies are necessary to implement for the safety and security of the networks. Secure password selection is one of the most important and easiest security measures. To select a secure password, a user should use at least eight to twenty-one alphanumeric characters and symbols, avoid obvious passwords, use invisible characters, and keep passwords private. As soon as a password is compromised, a user should notify the IT department and change the password.

Hardware and software maintenance is essential to ensure proper and efficient functioning of computer systems. Hardware maintenance includes cleaning all devices with appropriate cloths and solutions. Software maintenance includes running antivirus and antimalware programs to clean up the malicious software.

Software maintenance also includes installing and running a disk cleanup program that creates more storage space. More storage space can also be created by backing up hard drives and data. Critical OS updates are very important to install to ensure continuous compatibility of an OS with the running programs.

CASE STUDY

You are in charge of implementing security and maintenance procedures for the computer networks you designed for the case study at the end of chapter 4. Pick a specific classroom or lab set up with at least forty computers. Describe what countermeasures you plan to use to guard against physical security threats that can compromise network assets. Explain why. Also describe what countermeasures you plan to use to guard against software security threats that can compromise network assets. Explain why.

EXERCISES AND DISCUSSION QUESTIONS

1. Describe vulnerabilities for hardware and software.
2. Describe the advantages and disadvantages of qualitative and quantitative risk calculations for asset evaluations.
3. Define and explain the following: types of security threats, firewall, and VPN.
4. Describe layered security and explain how and why each layer is used.
5. Describe the hardening of the OS and give three examples of how it is achieved.

REFERENCES

Easttom, C. (2013). *Network defense and countermeasures: Principles and practices* (2nd Ed.). Upper Saddle River, NJ: Pearson Education.

Sims, S. (2012). *Qualitative vs. quantitative risk assessment.* Retrieved from http://www.sans.edu/research/leadership-laboratory/article/risk-assessment
Tyson, J., & Crawford, S. (2011). *How VPNs work.* Retrieved from http://computer.howstuffworks.com/vpn.htm

SEVEN

Teaching and Learning with Technology

OBJECTIVES

At the conclusion of the chapter, the reader will be able to:

1. Understand the main philosophical perspectives on using computer technologies for teaching and learning (ISTE 1, 2, 3, 4, 5, 6).
2. Explain the potential value added by various classes of technology to the teaching and learning process (ISTE 1, 2, 3, 5, 6).
3. Understand a general approach to integrating technology into teaching (ISTE 1, 2, 3, 4, 5, 6).
4. Describe various ways technologies can help support student learning activities (ISTE 1, 2, 3, 6).
5. Identify correct and incorrect ways to use technology with existing lessons (ISTE 1, 2, 3, 5, 6).
6. Describe some ways to enhance lessons with commonly available technology tools (ISTE 2, 3, 5, 6).

USING COMPUTER TECHNOLOGIES FOR TEACHING AND LEARNING

How does one effectively use technology to improve teaching and learning in the classroom? This is a key question posed by many teachers who want to use technology to improve teaching and learning in their classrooms. There are many books, journals, and even fields of scholarly study devoted to addressing this question. This chapter covers some of the basics of this topic. It also presents a way of thinking about how computer technologies can help improve teaching and learning. This can serve as a critical lens for thinking through ideas presented by numerous other texts and examples on this topic.

A simple cooking analogy can help begin to explain how technology can support learning. Imagine a man named Paul wishes to learn how to prepare crispy homemade potato chips. The process involves three basic steps: (1) Peel the potatoes, (2) cut the potatoes into thin slices, and (3) fry the slices. Imagine also that Paul has technology tools that can help with each step of this process. The tools can actually complete each step for Paul, and do so in much less time than a person performing the task manually.

Paul begins by performing each step manually to create his first batch of chips. Peeling takes ten minutes, cutting takes ten minutes, and frying takes ten minutes. The experience is fun, but the quality of the first batch is not quite right. Paul thinks that maybe his slicing skills need some work. But if he were to do everything manually again for another batch, it would take another thirty minutes.

So he decides to use his technology tools to help him. He has one technology tool to complete the potato peeling. He focuses on just slicing manually. Then he has another tool perform the frying for him. The peeling tool completes its task in just one minute, Paul slices in ten minutes, and the frying tool completes its task in one minute. Paul happily practices slicing for an hour.

If Paul had done everything manually without the technology tools, he would have completed only two additional practice batches during that hour. But by using his technology tools, Paul was able to complete five batches of chips, and practice slicing five times during the hour. The technology tools added value to his learning activities by allowing Paul to practice slicing five times instead of two times during the hour.

Philosophical Perspectives on Computer-based Technologies

There are different philosophical perspectives on how computer-based technologies should be used in education. Some try to view computer technologies as tools that can largely replace a human teacher. Instructional materials, activities, assessments of learning, and feedback are all provided by the technology tool. Computer-based training (CBT) and e-learning are examples of this approach (Nicholson, 2007). Many tutorial and "drill and practice" applications are also examples of this approach. Currently, companies like Litmos offer services to develop CBT units for corporations. They claim their services can improve internal training for employees by reducing time in classrooms and reducing training costs.

Others try to view computer technologies as tools to help teachers do their teaching more efficiently and effectively. Technology tools can help teachers facilitate class activities and prepare higher quality teaching materials more easily. Document production tools, learning management systems (LMSs), academic recording-keeping tools, instant feedback systems, and classroom hardware like video projectors and interactive whiteboards are all examples of teacher-supporting technology tools.

Still others argue that computer technologies should be viewed as tools primarily for supporting the learner (Papert, 1994). For example, Jonassen (2006) refers to technologies that students can use as "mindtools." In this view, technology tools primarily should be used to help support students' attempts to learn. Technology tools should help students grapple more effectively with the concepts being learned as they participate in learning activities like experimentation, research, discussion, and document production.

All three of these approaches have their place and can be used together in a classroom environment. Self-contained learning tools can be used within a larger curriculum that uses a variety of tools and approaches. An existing classroom lesson can be improved with the use of both teacher-focused and student-focused technology. Many tools, like document production and research tools, can be seen as tools for both teachers and students.

Computer Technologies Can Amplify

All basic technologies, from older paper, pencil, and overhead projector technologies, to modern wireless, networked, computer-based technologies, can be used to support almost any pedagogical approach. Teachers who prefer lecture-based instruction can use technology to create more polished-looking lecture materials, and even make their lectures available to students twenty-four hours a day through video and web technologies.

Teachers who prefer worksheet-based activities for learning can use technology to create and print worksheets faster than before. They can even make interactive electronic worksheets available to students at home through web technologies. Teachers who prefer student research-based activities can use technology to enable students to conduct research faster than was possible before the widespread use of the Internet. Teachers who prefer problem-based learning can generate more interesting problem scenario materials and make available a larger set of support resources by using computer technologies.

Each technology has certain affordances that make them more or less suited for certain tasks, but most technology tools are not inherently "constructivist," "didactic," or "behaviorist." While there are exceptions like CBTs (which have pedagogical approaches embedded in the design of the tool), technology tools in general are pedagogy-free and can be used to amplify the practice of almost any instructional approach. They can amplify the negative characteristics of a lesson design or amplify the positive characteristics of a lesson design.

The key, then, to using technology effectively is to first select an effective pedagogical approach for reaching a particular set of learning objectives, and then to use (or create) appropriate technology tools to enhance and strengthen parts of the lesson. Practically speaking, the process is not necessarily linear in this way either. Sometimes, the capabilities of an exciting technology tool can inspire a teacher to design new pedagogical approaches that take advantage of the features of the technology.

How Computer Technologies Amplify

A classic example of computational technology use in schools is that of calculators in mathematics and science courses. Calculators can perform large complex computations quickly and accurately. So, students can use calculators to perform the computations they encounter while solving a math or science problem. This allows them to focus their attention on the conceptual steps for solving the problem. Because math and science students can spend more time practicing the conceptual process of problem solving as a result, calculator use can lead to better math and science learning.

Computer-based technologies are more powerful than calculators and other older technologies that have traditionally been in use in schools (like film projectors, televisions, typewriters, and chalkboards). They share many of the positive features of these older technologies, but have some new features that make them especially powerful. Four areas that largely capture why computer technologies are an especially powerful class of tool include speed, multimodal input and output, high-quality output, and programmability.

Speed

Like calculators, computer technologies can perform tasks very quickly. Whether it has to do with performing mathematical computations, searching through records, sending and receiving large quantities of information, or applying special visual effects to photographs, computer technologies perform many information-processing-related tasks at incredible speeds. For almost any task, enabling students and teachers to perform the same tasks at a fraction of the usual time allows them to spend extra time on other productive learning activities.

Multimodal Input and Output

Computer technologies have the ability to present users with information through text, graphics, audio, and video. Computer technologies can also be used to accept input in multiple ways. These include the use of keyboards, microphones, still cameras, video cameras, joysticks, and other devices. This flexibility enables computer technologies to be used for a broad range of tasks.

High-Quality Output

A large variety of high-quality products (whether printed documents, graphics, music, etc.) can be easily created with modern computer technologies. Photo books, for example, can be created on computers for a fraction of the cost, time, and energy that used to be required prior to the proliferation of modern desktop publishing and photo editing software.

Presentation slides of high visual quality incorporating text and color graphics used to require professional publishing tools. Now even elementary school students can create them easily. Professional-looking video clips can be created using a cell phone camera and free video editing software. This ability to create high-quality products can be motivating for teachers and students.

Programmability

Combined with the previously described features, programmability is probably the key feature that makes computer technologies special. A programmable tool is a flexible tool that can be expanded and modified to fit the needs of users. A programmable tool also enables the creation of interactive applications.

These can range from simple multiplication drill-and-practice software (e.g., Math Blaster) to complex interactive environments for exploring geometric concepts (e.g., Geometer Sketchpad). There are even sophisticated applications that enable the exploration of physics concepts (e.g., PhET Interactive Simulations) and historical events and situations (e.g., National Geographic's The Underground Railroad: Journey to Freedom).

Combining these capabilities has led to the creation of a broad range of computer-based technology tools that have the potential to add a lot of value to teaching and learning. Later sections of this chapter highlight the value provided by various categories of computer-based technology tools in greater detail.

Controlling Complexity and Scaffolding

As mentioned earlier, with some exceptions, most computer technologies are pedagogy free and can be used to amplify the practice of almost any instructional approach. Those using lectures can produce lectures of higher quality and produce them more quickly. Those relying on writing tasks (or other document production) can allow students to use technology tools to create documents faster and of potentially higher quality. Those using research activities can also enable students to conduct more comprehensive research.

The amplification of teaching practices can also occur through the enabling of flexible complexity control and scaffolding. Controlling complexity is the idea that students may be better able to learn something that is very complex if the instructor strategically removes and introduces complexities in an appropriate way. Activities and instruction can be sequenced to have the complexity gradually increased as they become more comfortable with various skills and concepts.

For example, for students learning to drive a car, merging onto a busy expressway is not one of the first maneuvers they are asked to try. Instead students are first taught smaller simple tasks like accelerating and stopping smoothly. Then they may learn to make turns safely. After that, they may learn to change lanes in light and slow traffic conditions. Eventually, after students master the easier skills, they will attempt to merge onto a busy expressway.

Complexity is controlled in this example through a sensible simple-to-hard sequencing of skills to be learned. Students are asked to master smaller component skills before even attempting the more complex skills. However, this is not the only way to control complexity.

Scaffolding is the idea that a teacher can help students learn by having them complete some interesting whole task very early on. This is done at the beginning with temporary support being provided to the student. Then gradually over time, the support is removed until independence is eventually achieved. This approach is often used when learning a particular skill or concept that is more motivating and interesting within the context of a larger whole task.

Scaffolding once again is an example of controlling complexity. When scaffolding, a teacher is reducing the overall complexity of a task and enabling a student to focus on a smaller part of the task. The student still participates in the larger task to sustain interest and motivation. When the scaffolding is gradually removed, the teacher is gradually increasing the overall complexity of the task, at a rate that is manageable for the student. The initial reduction of complexity, and the gradual increase at an appropriate rate, supports the ability of a student to perform and learn components of the whole task.

As an example, consider a geometry unit about area and volume with students who have weak computational skills. A teacher may choose to control complexity for these students by allowing them to use a calculator for computations. This would enable them to grapple with area and volume concepts without worrying about getting the multiplication wrong. This can reduce frustration for students and enable them to participate and learn more confidently. Use of a calculator in this example reduces complexity for students by scaffolding their weak computational skills.

Once again, controlling complexity is a broad idea. It is an important but sometimes very tricky idea to apply. For example, if the math unit being taught is about two-digit addition, one could reasonably ask, should students be allowed to use calculators? If yes, then when and why? Sometimes it is difficult to know when and where the complexity should be reduced to promote learning.

To answer this particular question, going back to the cooking analogy presented earlier can help. Paul wanted to learn to be better at slicing potatoes. He reduced the complexity of the potato chip cooking task by using technology tools to take care of the other steps, peeling and frying. This allowed him to focus on the slicing. Reducing the surrounding complexity allowed him to focus more time and attention on learning about performing the potato slicing component well.

However, if Paul had instead used his technology tools to take care of all three steps, (peeling, slicing, and frying) Paul would have created batches of chips even more quickly. But he would not have learned how to improve his potato slicing skills. His use of technology tools would have taken away the wrong type of complexity. Basically, instead of supporting his learning of potato slicing by reducing the surrounding complexity, it would have removed the target slicing complexity altogether by performing all the slicing for him.

Applying this way of thinking to calculators and two-digit addition, if students simply punched in all the numbers and hit the plus button, they would turn in all correct answers on their assignments. However, they potentially would not have learned anything about two-digit addition. Instead of supporting student learning of two-digit addition, the calculator technology in this approach would be doing the two-digit addition work for them. This use of calculators does not help students learn.

As mentioned earlier, the key to designing effective technology-enhanced lessons is to have a solid pedagogical plan. It is possible to have a two-digit addition unit with a plan where calculators do indeed help.

It may involve activities where students think through graphic representations of two-digit addition and procedural elements of performing two-digit addition first, and then calculators can be used to provide fast feedback when checking manual addition work. The crucial point here is that the technology enables students to *focus their attention* on the critical area of complexity rather than *removing* the critical area of complexity.

It was noted earlier in this chapter, that sometimes the pedagogy is chosen first, and then the technology. At other times, the strong features of a technology inspire a novel pedagogical plan. With either approach, it is helpful to understand how various types of technology tools are generally useful. How are some currently popular tools particularly helpful and what are some common situations when they may be used? How do various types of technology tools tend to add value? Understanding these capabilities will help a teacher use technology more effectively to enhance teaching and learning. The next section of this chapter addresses this.

In addition, with each technology tool, some examples of appropriate use are shared. The examples are based on pedagogical approaches with an existing strong research base. It is not within the scope of this chapter to go into these in great depth, but they are provided as a reference. The approaches include:

- Learning through problem solving
- Learning through model building
- Learning through anchored instruction
- Learning in community
- Learning in knowledge-building communities

CONSTRUCTION TOOLS

Construction tools are one of the broadest categories of computer technology based tools available. Teachers use these tools to create teaching materials. Students use them to create documents for assignments. Their use is wide-ranging and flexible. Word processors, presentation programs, paint programs, and video editors are some examples of technology tools that can be used to create or "construct" things.

Word Processors

Word processing programs provide an interactive environment for creating text documents with many useful features. They enable the easy entry of text and changing of text features like font type, font size, margins, and spacing. They offer many other useful writing features as well,

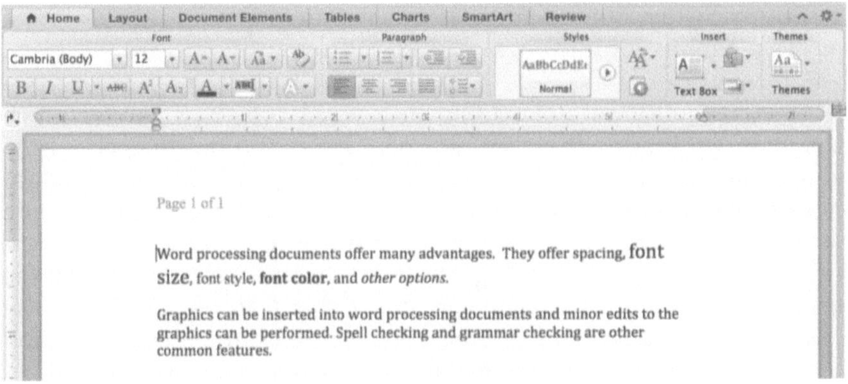

Figure 7.1. Example of a word processing document.

like automatic page numbering and spelling checks. All of them can save and print, while some word processors enable saving to special formats like PDF and HTML.

Word processors are available from multiple companies and include programs like Microsoft's Word, Corel's Word Perfect, and Apple's Pages. While they can be purchased separately, word processing programs are often offered as part of an "office" suite of productivity tools that include presentation, spreadsheet, and email programs. Each looks slightly different, but most word processors share the same basic typing and editing features. Figure 7.1 shows an example of a word processing document screen in Word.

Most word processing programs save files in their own specific format, but many of them can open and save in other application formats. Free office software suites are also available for most computer platforms. Examples include Apache, OpenOffice, LibreOffice, and NeoOffice.

Value Added by Word Processors

Good lesson designs that require student writing can be enhanced through the use of word processing tools. Word processors as technology tools can add value in many ways. Assuming students have the requisite typing and basic computer skills, a simple substitution of a word processing tool for paper and pen use can lead to many benefits such as:

- Faster text entry and editing of text features like fonts, spacing, margins, and other design elements
- Special language features like spell check, grammar check, and thesaurus

- Easy inclusion of graphics from other sources
- High-quality output

To begin, composition and editing in a word processor can be much faster than working with paper and pen. Fonts can be changed easily, and spacing for an entire document can be changed in seconds. Special language features like spell checking and grammar checking can provide scaffolding to younger writers who are still working on their mechanics. More time can be spent thinking about the content than working on the mechanics of writing neatly and correctly. Other features, like the ability to easily add graphics and photographs, can encourage creativity and lead to visually attractive final documents. Students may be more willing to show and share their work when it looks attractive.

Cloud-based Word Processors

Most word processing programs are installed and run on a single computer. However, another class of word processors is now available through companies offering services through the World Wide Web. Google, for example, offers an "office" suite of tools that run through a web browser and store files on its company file servers. The word processor in this suite is called Google Docs. It offers most of the basic features of other word processors including standard text font, spacing, pagination, and spelling tools (figure 7.2).

With tools that are offered through web browsers, most of the storage and computational processing are performed on the service company's computers. As a result, they are also known as *online* services or *cloud-based* services. Google Docs is an example of a cloud-based word proces-

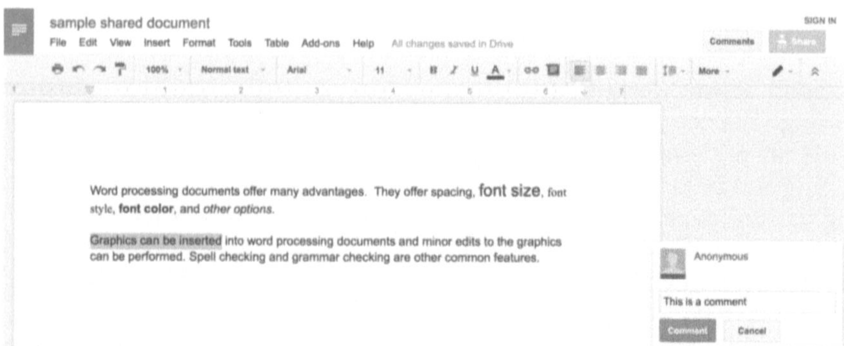

Figure 7.2. Example of a Google Docs cloud-based word processing document.

sor. Being cloud-based enables Google Docs and other similar online tools, to provide some powerful additional features. They include:

- Multiuser access
- Multiplatform access
- Simultaneous access
- Cloud-based storage

A Google doc can be "shared" with multiple users, giving them read-only, comment-only, or full editing access (figure 7.3). Wikis and blogs also allow multiuser access, but generally only permit document editing by one person at a time. A Google Doc, on the other hand, permits simultaneous editing by multiple users. Several users can type, read, and add comments at the same time, and all users see the changes in real time on their screens.

This highly responsive interactivity opens up many possibilities for collaborative work on written documents. Collaborative work on documents with traditional word processors, involved sending files back and forth and keeping track of who made what changes and when. The ability to work on a single, online document greatly simplifies the collaborative work process.

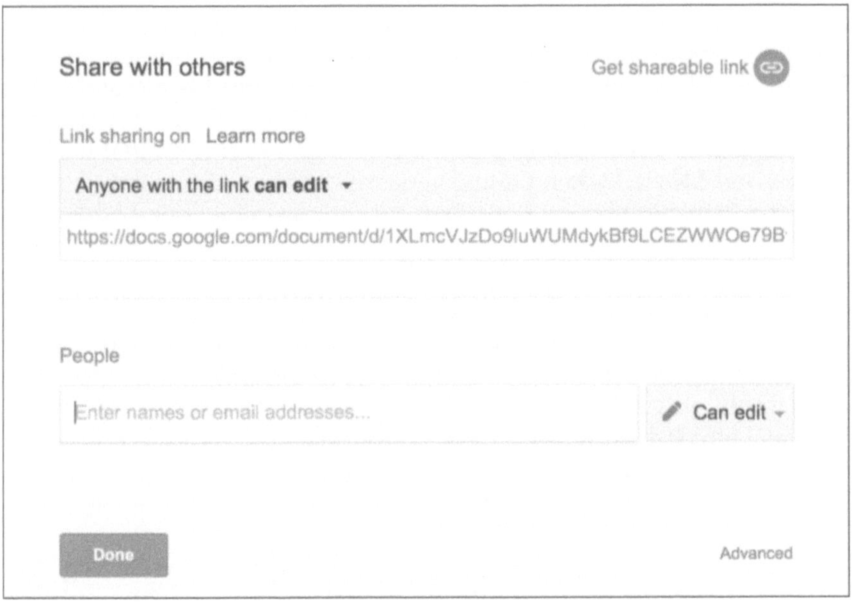

Figure 7.3. Example of Google Docs "sharing with others" window.

In addition, documents are saved "in the cloud" and can be accessed with devices from multiple platforms including desktops, tablets, and even smartphones. So access to the documents is possible from school, at home, or even on the road. This flexible access enables the extension of schoolwork outside of school walls. There is no need to worry about forgetting a storage device like a USB flash drive at home or at school. Access to a shared document is available from almost anywhere the web can be accessed.

There are some negatives to cloud-based word processing. First of all, access to the Internet is required to do any work. Second, when a network connection is slow, work on a document can at times feel sluggish and unresponsive. The network bandwidth requirements for word processing tend to be low. But for cloud-based services that handle graphics, audio, or video, this network limitation can become significant.

Other Traditional and Cloud-based Tools

Like the word processing example, presentation programs, graphics programs, and video-editing programs introduce similar efficiencies and advantages for their respective document domains. There are also cloud-based equivalents for presentations, graphics, and video. Those also introduce similar conveniences and restrictions.

Popular presentation programs include PowerPoint, Keynote, and OpenOffice. Online versions of presentation tools include Google Presentation, Prezi, and Haiku Deck. Popular graphics programs include Photoshop, Photoshop Elements, Paintshop Pro, Sketchbook, and GIMP. Online versions of graphics programs include Pixlr Editor and Sumo Paint. Popular video editing programs include Premiere, Final Cut Pro, iMovie, and Movie Maker. Online versions of video editing programs include YouTube Editor and WeVideo, but they are slower and have fewer features.

The network speed (or bandwidth) requirements are significantly greater for graphics and video tools. Practically speaking, intensive work with the editing of graphics or video is not advisable with cloud-based tools; it would be too slow. Consequently, some online video programs for example, only offer very basic editing features and none of the powerful visual effects features offered by traditional video editing programs.

Construction Tools for Supporting Learning Designs

As mentioned earlier, in any good lesson design where writing is required, a word processor can be used as a faster, more reliable, and more motivating document creation tool substitute. Similarly, presentation programs, graphics programs, and video editing programs can also be used as substitutes with extra features for their respective document types.

In "learning through model building" lesson designs, where student-constructed documents can be models (or representations) of what students are learning, construction tools can help in many ways. They can be used to create more interesting models with the broad variety of media options available through computer-based construction tools. The higher quality products can lead to greater motivation for some students.

Construction tools can also be used to more quickly create various documents and media. The time saved by tool use can be reallocated for other sense-making activities like additional research or more frequent model revision. Cloud-based versions of construction tools, which usually make collaborative work and document sharing easier, could lead to additional modifications of the lesson design. More student collaboration could be encouraged during model construction, and more thorough peer evaluation and critique could be added to the design.

In lesson designs influenced by "learning through knowledge-building communities," the ability to share knowledge is especially important. When cloud-based word processing tools are used, students can create documents and share them very easily with the rest of the class. Both students and teachers can quickly view and comment on contributions to the shared knowledge base, thereby encouraging more frequent peer critique. Management of documents is greatly simplified (no need for a central database program) and teachers are free to focus more attention on providing good feedback than on keeping track of documents and databases.

ANALYSIS AND VISUALIZATION TOOLS

The ability of computers to perform computations very rapidly has led to the development of tools to assist in the analysis of data. Coupled with a computer's ability to project images on large color displays, there are many tools that help create and display graphic representations of information. These representations are sometimes called *visualizations*.

Some tools are general-purpose data analysis programs like spreadsheet and database software. Others are specialized programs that display only certain types of data like weather maps and stock market performance graphs. Some incorporate simulations of physical or social events, and enable the analysis and visualization of information related to these simulated events. These tools together have many applications for teaching and learning.

Spreadsheets

A strong example of a flexible computer-based tool that helps with analysis and visualization is spreadsheet software. Spreadsheet programs provide an interactive environment for aggregating and analyzing information. Most use a standard table interface with rows and columns, where users can enter numbers, text, and other information in "cells." Figure 7.4 shows an example of a spreadsheet screen with its tabular organization of data.

Along with displaying information in an organized way, spreadsheets allow users to perform computations with the information. For example, row 18 of figure 7.4 shows a series of cells where the average of the upper cells has been computed for each column. An average is just one of the many computations spreadsheets can perform. Large libraries of mathematical, statistical, string, and logical functions are available in most spreadsheet packages.

Spreadsheets can also be used to generate graphic representations of data. Figure 7.5 shows an example of a simple bar graph that can be generated with a spreadsheet program. Bar graphs, pie charts, line graphs, and scatterplots are among the many types of graphs that most spreadsheets can generate.

Like other products mentioned so far, spreadsheet programs are available from many companies and include Microsoft's Excel and Apple's Numbers. Spreadsheets are often included as part of an "office" suite of tools; there are free spreadsheets available as a part of free office suites in-

	A	B	C	D	E	F	G	H	I
1									
2									
3		GENDER	HW 1	HW 2	TEST 1	HW 3	HW 4	TEST 2	
4		F	80	88	96	99	73	80	
5		F	86	79	99	85	80	79	
6		M	96	95	100	73	79	95	
7		F	99	63	99	80	95	84	
8		F	100	86	85	79	63	95	
9		F	99	84	73	95	73	95	
10		M	85	84	80	84	80	63	
11		M	73	96	79	84	79	86	
12		F	80	99	95	96	95	80	
13		M	67	75	63	99	95	79	
14		M	79	88	86	75	63	95	
15		F	72	94	79	88	86	95	
16		M	80	84	93	94	84	86	
17									
18		AVERAGES	84.3	85.8	86.7	87.0	80.4	85.5	
19									

Figure 7.4. Example of a spreadsheet screen.

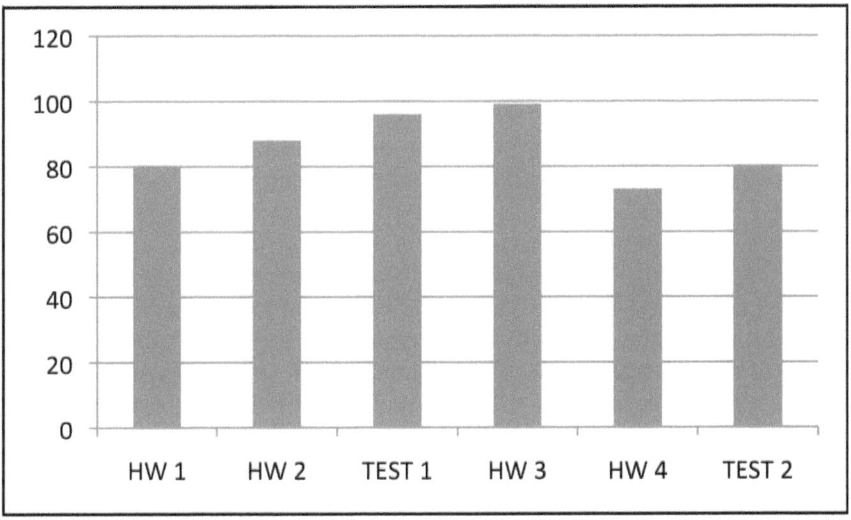

Figure 7.5. Example of a simple bar graph.

cluding OpenOffice, LibreOffice, and NeoOffice. Online spreadsheet programs like Google Spreadsheet are available as part of their cloud-based office services suite too. Cloud-based spreadsheets have the same kind of advantages and disadvantages that cloud-based word processors and presentation programs have compared to their traditional counterparts.

Value Added by Spreadsheets

Existing good lesson designs that require data analysis can be enhanced through the use of analysis and visualization tools like spreadsheets. Spreadsheets can add value to a lesson in many ways. A substitution of a spreadsheet tool for paper, pen, and calculator tools, can lead to many benefits such as:

- Fast data entry speed
- Fast, easily repeatable performance of computations on data, including complex mathematical, logical, and statistical computations
- Easy management of large sets of data
- Easy creation of graphs and charts
- High quality output

To begin, data entry into a spreadsheet by typing manually is straightforward. Data from other electronic sources can be imported into spreadsheets fairly easily too. Once the data are entered, performing computations like averages and sums is extremely fast. Complex formulas constructed for computing some quantity, can easily be copied and pasted to other parts of the spreadsheet to perform the same computations for other sets of numbers. If one or many data values in cells are changed for an existing computed quantity, recomputing occurs almost instantly.

The ability to generate many different types of *graphs* accurately is another strong feature of spreadsheets. Sometimes, there may be relationships in a set of data that are hard to notice by just looking at the numbers in a table. However, a visual representation of that data can help users more quickly see trends and other relationships, especially in large sets of data. Spreadsheets enable the fast, easy creation of such visualizations.

The benefits of these features are easy to see in mathematics and science classes. For example, in science, a computation requiring ten steps may need to be repeated over and over for many sets of data. Performing these computations manually, or even with the help of a calculator, can take a very long time.

Setting up the computations once using a spreadsheet, and then having the spreadsheet repeat the computations with different data sets, saves a lot of time. This enables students to spend more time and energy on understanding conceptual ideas of the task. Put another way, spreadsheets can reduce the complexity associated with repeatedly performing calculations accurately, allowing students to focus more attention on other complexities related to interpreting the data.

Furthermore, the process of constructing formulas within a spreadsheet can also help draw students' attention to understanding concepts related to the algorithms themselves. Some teaching approaches like learning through modeling claim that the constructed formulas and data arrangements in a spreadsheet are themselves "models" of a student's understanding of a problem and of how it should be solved.

Students can focus on revising and refining their models, because their cognitive energies do not need to be used on the detailed mechanics of the actual individual computations being performed over and over on different sets of numbers. In other words, spreadsheets help reduce the complexity of one part of the problem-solving task (the numerical computations). This allows students to focus their attention on the complexity of another part of the problem-solving task (the modeling of the conceptual steps).

Special Purpose Analysis and Visualization Tools

While spreadsheets are a flexible tool that can be used to interactively analyze and visualize any set of data, there are also tools that are dedicated to:

1. Helping users create certain specific types of visualizations
2. Helping users analyze and visualize certain specific types of data
3. Helping users analyze and visualize relationships in certain specific situations

Each of these specialized tools provide quicker access and interaction with data than a more general-purpose tool like a spreadsheet program. However, this specialization also limits their usability for purposes other than the ones they were specifically designed to address.

In the first category, there are tools like Inspiration, Bubbl.us, and Cmap, which are dedicated concept-mapping tools. Concept maps are one type of visualization (figure 7.6). They attempt to provide a visual representation of ideas with boxes and lines that help show relationships between ideas.

Many lesson designs use concept-mapping activities and dedicated concept-mapping tools offer advantages over paper-based concept mapping. Advantages include map creation speed, map editing speed, graphics options, printing options, and sharing options. It should be noted that while concept maps can be created with other software tools like word processors and paint programs, concept-mapping tools provide specialized support specifically for creating and managing concept maps more efficiently.

In the second category, there are dedicated programs designed to help show visualizations of specific types of data. For example, opening up a weather application or visiting a weather-related website (e.g., weather.com) reveals visualizations like temperature maps, precipitation maps, wind speed maps, and cloud cover animations. Some of this information, like temperature variations over a geographic area, can't really be

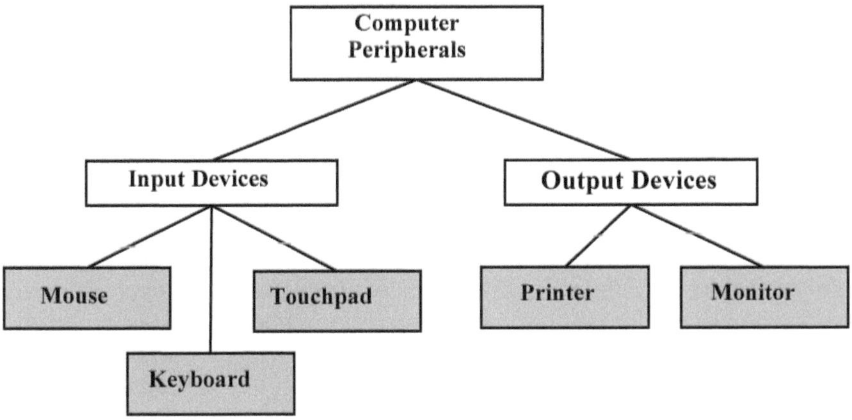

Figure 7.6. Example of a concept map

"seen" in the real world. But representing temperature data with colors and spreading them over a geographic map helps people see patterns in spatial temperature distributions.

Another example can be seen when visiting a financial website. Tools that provide interactive access to performance graphs of indexes like the Dow Jones Industrial Average are available for use. The visualization tools help users see trends and activity in the stock market. There are also websites that provide access to interactive tools for viewing social data like population, income, and carbon emission information. These, and other tools, can be used to improve learning activities that promote a conceptual understanding of relationships in science, economics, and social studies.

In the third category are dedicated programs designed to help users analyze and visualize relationships in certain specific situations. Science simulations and social simulations of specific situations fit into this category. For example, there are many physics and chemistry simulations available freely from websites like the PhET website of the University of Colorado Boulder.

A simulation of gas being compressed in a cylinder provides an interactive animation that shows the increasing motion of gas molecules as the volume in the cylinder is reduced by a piston. Individual gas molecules cannot be seen in the real world. However, the simulation shows graphic representations of gas molecules to help students "see" the change in gas molecule activity. In this specific visualization, being able to see an interactive animation of moving gas molecules can help students develop a stronger intuitive understanding of why when volume is decreased, gas pressure increases (molecules hit and bounce off the cylinder walls more frequently as volume decreases).

In this gas molecule example, the simulation tool does something more than offer speed advantages or reduced task complexity. Instead, it provides students with a previously unavailable ability that has the potential to be very helpful; the simulation allows students to "look inside" to see the underlying molecular interactions. The benefit of this is somewhat like having a person stick his hand in a black bag of one hundred marbles to try to find the one blue marble. Then, imagine how helpful it would be if the bag were instead transparent, allowing the person to look inside.

Another good interactive simulation shows waves propagating along a string (figure 7.7). It shows the effects of changing string characteristics like tension and of changing wave oscillation characteristics like amplitude and frequency. In this specific situation, unlike the gas cylinder example, most of what is shown in the simulation can actually be seen in

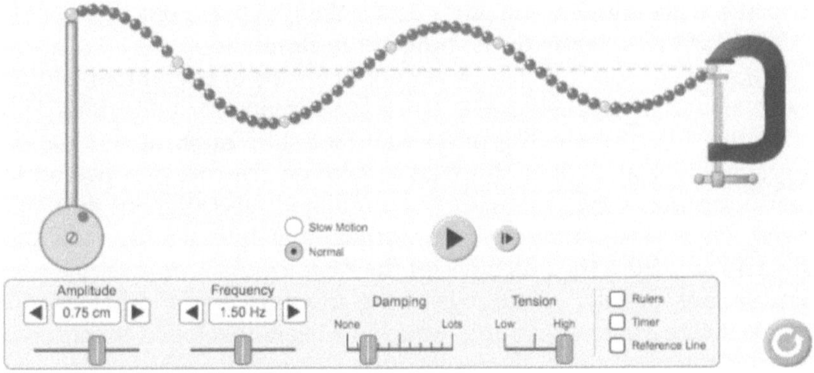

Figure 7.7. Simulation of waves propagating along a string. (Courtesy of PhET™ Interactive Simulations, University of Colorado, http://phet.colorado.edu.)

a physical demonstration of waves on a string. A physics instructor, with a sufficient budget to purchase equipment and materials, can set this up in front of the classroom for all too see and make the same changes represented in the simulation.

One of the values of this particular simulation is that teachers can have students experiment with the waves on a string on their own. Instead of having to take turns on one apparatus in the front of the class, students can individually explore changes with various factors and see the outcomes at their desks. Also, instead of being forced to see only a few examples during limited class time, the visualization tool helps students see what happens as many times as they want inside and outside of class. This particular simulation adds value by giving students longer individual opportunities to analyze and see various changes.

In the case of this science simulation, some task complexity is decreased by the tool. For example, the complexity of having to set up and maintain the experimental apparatus is greatly reduced by the use of a simulation. The simulation tool requires very little set up. This allows students to spend more time on other sense-making parts of the task.

The wave simulation can also add "look inside" type value for a student. For example, the animation on the screen can be slowed down to help students see how wave variations travel down the string as oscillation frequency and amplitude are dynamically modified. It is very hard to slow down wave propagation in the real world. A person could video record the wave motion and slow down the playback, but this is not as easy a process as slowing down time in the simulation.

Simulations of social scenarios are another type of useful tool, but they are not as widely available as science simulations for educators. However, some, like the Underground Railroad simulation at the National Geographic website, allow students to take on the role of a person in a scenario. Students interact with the simulated environment and make choices. They learn through the informational interactions with other characters and from the outcomes of their choices.

Simulations developed for e-learning modules are another example (Schank, 2002). Many e-learning units have been developed for corporate and educational settings. Examples include providing customer service skills training for new company employees and learning how to write a business document.

COMMUNICATION AND COLLABORATION TOOLS

Computer technologies can be used to send and receive information very quickly. This has led to the development of many computer-based communication tools. Coupled with a computer's ability to use multimodal channels (text, graphics, sound, video, etc.), there are computer tools for enabling users to communicate in a variety of ways like sending instant text messages, sharing picture files, and even talking to someone in real time with audio and video.

Collaboration is a social practice that can be done without technology tools. However, the flexibility and speed provided by computer-based communication tools support better collaboration. Some communication tools have been combined with other construction tool features to create tools focused specifically on supporting collaborative work. These communication and collaboration tools can be very useful for supporting teaching and learning.

Examples of communication tools include email, web browsers, the World Wide Web itself, file transfer tools, online meeting tools, and LMSs. Most of these computer-based communication tools use the Internet to send and receive information. Email, file transfer protocol, and the World Wide Web were built as a layer of services on top of the Internet.

The World Wide Web

The practice of viewing content from the World Wide Web (also "WWW" or just the "web") has become so common and widespread, that there are short phrases and abbreviations that have become a regular part of our everyday language. Phrases like, "web browsing," "surfing the web," and "web research" are readily understood by most people.

The World Wide Web is basically a network of computers connected to the Internet that are also running software that enables them to provide web services—hence these computers become "web servers." The web was invented in 1989 by Tim Berners-Lee who was working at the European Organization for Nuclear Research. It was useful primarily for the scientific community it served (Berners-Lee & Fischetti, 1999).

The web has grown significantly since then in many ways. The technical features of the web certainly grew over time, but two developments really made the web useful to the general public: (1) the growth of a large volume of useful information and (2) the growth of services to enable people to quickly search that large volume of information.

Content originally made available on the web was specialized scientific content for a scientific community. As other entities started providing free content, the web became useful for a much larger community. These other entities included universities, libraries, government agencies, corporations, magazines, and news agencies. Today, having a web presence is assumed as necessary for any business, government agency, nonprofit organization, educational institution, or social organization that aims to be viewed as legitimate.

But having a lot of content available is only useful if people can find the content they need quickly and easily. Online search engine services developed by companies like Yahoo, Google, Microsoft, and a host of others provide this essential service. Vast useful content and usable searching combined, provide us now with the ability to do productive "web research." We have reached a point where visiting a physical library has become almost unnecessary for many research tasks.

Web browsers, web servers, and search engines provide us with a foundational set of technology tools to support highly efficient synchronous and asynchronous communication. A large number of other communication and collaboration tools are built with or on top of this foundation. Examples of additional tools include instant messaging, discussion boards, blogs, wikis, LMSs, cloud-based document construction, online media sharing, and social media sites.

Value Added by Communication and Collaboration Tools

Existing good lesson designs that require research or collaboration can be enhanced through the use of communication and collaboration technology tools. Adding technology-enabled choices like web research as an option on top of library research, or cloud-based document construction as an option on top of face-to-face group work, can lead to many benefits such as:

- Faster information access
- Access to a larger repositories of information
- Twenty-four-hour access to many resources
- Easier and more flexible document sharing
- Flexible conversation options
- Flexible feedback options

To begin, finding information through web research is often significantly faster than going to a library and searching manually through physical print materials. Information from online publications can be found in seconds compared with the many minutes or hours it may take to find the same information from print versions of the same publications.

On top of that, the sheer quantity of information that is accessible through the web is larger than any local library could hope to house. There are physical limitations to local libraries holding print materials, while the web enables access to public information anywhere in the world. Online web resources also tend to remain available continuously. Web research can be done early in the morning, during the day, or late at night.

For teachers and students wishing to make documents available to others, web technologies enable many easy ways to freely post and share all kinds of files. A teacher can post a handout file on Google Drive and share the URL with her students. A student can record and post a video where he solves a math problem and share it easily with the teacher and other students through service providers like Educreations or YouTube.

Students wishing to have a conversation about a group project can not only discuss things face to face at school, they can also talk synchronously outside of school in group video-conferencing sessions. Free services like Google Hangouts enable group video-conferencing from students' homes. Other popular online meeting tools that are available for a fee include Adobe Connect, Cisco WebEx, and SABA. Many of these tools offer the ability to broadcast audio, broadcast video, display presentations, share documents, share a common whiteboard screen, and even record meetings.

Learning Management Systems

It is possible for teachers to create their own web pages and post them on school web servers or free commercial web hosting services. Teachers can also find free discussion board services to host online discussions about topics that extend beyond the confines of the classroom. Resourceful teachers can find and cobble together a set of services to support communication and collaboration activities on their own.

LMSs can simplify work for teachers and students by providing common online services useful for education in one integrated package. Some examples of popular LMSs include Blackboard, Moodle, Sakai, and Schoology. Free and fee-based versions of these LMS services are typically available. Most LMSs allow teachers and students to do at least the following:

- Create simple web pages with text and graphics.
- Share documents, pictures, video, website links, and so on.
- Host moderated and open discussion boards.
- Support blog and wiki creation.
- Send secure messages to individuals or to groups of students.
- Manage assignment submission.
- Support grading processes with tools like clickable rubrics and feedback tracking.

LMSs allow teachers to extend the existing classroom environment with tools to create and support asynchronous online learning environments. For example, teachers can post instructional videos, homework exercises, and other support resources related to content for a given week on a class LMS site that is accessible at all hours from any location with web access. Students can access resources and participate in learning activities on their own time outside of class.

Numerous higher educational institutions are using LMSs to build fully online courses that provide multimedia content, interactive media, student assignments, online discussions, and assessments in one place. Many of these are aimed at college and adult learners primarily, but can be used for free. Large versions of these online classes are called *massive open online courses* (MOOCs). Some MOOCs have hundreds of students enrolled simultaneously. Examples of organizations that provide MOOCs include edX.org and Coursera.org.

The use of MOOCs and various cloud learning communities from many public and private cloud communities continues to grow. Both traditional and nontraditional institutions have offered open online courses and programs. Most of these MOOC programs are convenient and are offered at lowered costs for students. Some institutions have offered these open-education programs to the general public and are sharing their intellectual content for free.

While these programs continue to expand and improve on quality and capacity, significant time and resources are often required by the institutions to support them. Therefore, institutions need to be prudent in maintaining sufficient modern technology and effective formats for delivering information to the students. Also, while there have been some technological challenges, some students may need extra personal support because the online learning experience requires more independent initiative.

SPECIALIZED TEACHING AND LEARNING TOOLS

Many technology tools provide open-ended utility like office software and online communication tools. However, many specialized packages of computer tools also help support the learning of skills and content in specific areas, or help support certain steps of the teaching and learning process.

For example, as mentioned previously, all-encompassing learning systems that include curriculum, activities, and technology in one package are available for many subject areas. There are laboratory science kits with electronic sensors and probes connected to data collecting software that are available from companies like Pasco Scientific and Vernier. Math learning systems that provide a personalized sequence of instruction, activities, and assessments are available from companies like Carnegie Learning.

There are many assessment-focused technology tools and services available. They include traditional testing services as well as adaptive online testing systems that claim to offer better assessment through a personalized sequence of assessment questions. Technology-based assessment tools are available from organizations like the Northwest Evaluation Association (MAP), Scantron (Performance Series), and Goldstar Learning (Mastery Manager).

Each of these types of tools offers their own set of benefits and limitations. Many provide useful instructional support, but may require heavy use of school computing resources. Some are very expensive or require a service subscription from a school district. Users of these more specific technology tools should carefully evaluate the potential value added by these tools, in light of instructional goals and preferred pedagogical approaches.

SUMMARY

There are three main philosophical perspectives on the use of computer-based technologies in schools. One perspective views computer technologies as tools to replace human teachers. Another sees computer technologies as tools to help teachers teach more effectively. The third views computer technologies as tools primarily to help learners learn more effectively. These different perspectives can be used together in a classroom environment to improve the teaching and learning that occurs in schools.

Technologies often work by amplifying the abilities of teachers and students. For example, teachers who like to use lectures can produce lectures more efficiently. Students conducting research can perform research faster and more comprehensively with technology tools. Technologies have certain features that make them more or less suited for certain tasks, but most technology tools are not inherently "constructivist," "didactic," or "behaviorist."

The key to using technology effectively, then, is to select an appropriate pedagogical approach for reaching a particular set of learning objectives, and then using appropriate technology tools to enhance and strengthen parts of the lesson. Computer technologies are especially potent amplifiers because of four features: speed, multimodal input and output, high-quality output, and programmability. These features introduce efficiencies, enable flexible interactions, and can lead to greater student motivation.

One important way computer technologies help amplify is through their ability to support complexity control—and in particular scaffolding. Scaffolding is the idea that a teacher can help students learn by having them complete some interesting whole task very early on with temporary support. Gradually, over time, the support is removed until students achieve independence. Computer technologies can provide scaffolding in many subject areas including math, science, language arts, and social studies.

Construction tools are one category of computer technologies. They add value to a learning experience by enabling users to create and build things more efficiently. Word processors, presentation programs, and video editors are examples of these. Cloud-based word processors offer additional value by enabling multiple users to collaboratively write, critique, and edit a document in real time.

Analysis and visualization tools are another category of computer technologies. They add value in a number of ways. For example, spreadsheets are a tool in this category; they allow users to organize and produce graphic representations of data very quickly. Other visualization tools include specialized applications for creating concept maps and analyzing weather data.

Simulations also provide analytic and visual power by allowing users to control various factors of a physical experiment like time and spatial magnification. These enable users to "see" useful aspects of a physical event that would be difficult to notice in a real-world experiment.

Simulations of social scenarios also add value by allowing users to learn by performing virtual tasks in simulated social environments.

Examples of communication and collaboration tools include email and the World Wide Web. These tools enable the rapid search and retrieval of large volumes of information. Tasks involving research are made significantly easier by modern communication tools. There are also specialized technology tools that offer support for assessment, repetitive skill practice, and enhanced interactions with the real world. Each of these, when paired with an appropriate pedagogical approach, can add a lot of value to teaching and learning activities.

CASE STUDY

You are a technology integration coach at a school. Two departments have asked for your assistance. You are tasked with helping these departments understand how to integrate new technologies into their curriculum and to suggest some concrete next steps.

The science department chair recently went to a conference and saw some interesting demonstrations of computer-based sensors and probes. He has wanted members of his department to use more constructivist approaches to teaching chemistry. Currently about half lean toward constructivist approaches while half lean toward more didactic approaches. He wants to buy several sets of these sensors and probes and pass them out to every chemistry teacher.

He asks you for your opinion on this plan. Will this necessarily lead to the adoption of more constructivist teaching approaches? Why or why not? If yes, how might the new tools enable this? If no, what should the chair do instead to promote the increased use of constructivist teaching approaches?

The social studies department has noticed that students seem unmotivated, often turning in low-quality papers with minimal content. Teachers in the department would like to redesign their lessons to motivate students and to help students improve the academic content of their work. There are many ways to approach this, but the department would like to begin by trying to (1) encourage students to work collaboratively on assignments and to (2) provide students with additional work options that might be more interesting than just papers.

The teachers ask you for your advice. First of all, what kinds of technology tools might support collaborative student work? Secondly, what kinds of tools could be used to provide students with additional work options? The teachers would also like to know if you think they should take their existing lessons and simply insert the use of the new tools, or if they should instead try to completely redesign their lessons. What would your advice be? Why?

EXERCISES AND DISCUSSION QUESTIONS

1. What are the three main philosophical perspectives on the use of technology in schools?
2. What are some ways that computer technologies can amplify the work of teachers? What are some ways that computer technologies can amplify the efforts of students?
3. How should a teacher attempt to integrate technology into an existing lesson? How should a teacher attempt to integrate technology into a newly designed unit for some learning objective?
4. How do construction tools add value for a teacher or for a learner? What additional value is offered by cloud-based versions of construction tools?
5. What are the different ways that analysis and visualization tools can help learners?
6. How do communication and collaboration tools enable better collaboration?
7. Do technology tools necessarily work better with any particular pedagogical perspective? Why or why not?

REFERENCES

Berners-Lee, T., & Fischetti, M. (1999). *Weaving the web: The original design and ultimate destiny of the World Wide Web*. New York: Harper Collins.

Jonassen, D. (2006). *Modeling with technology: Mindtools for conceptual change*. Upper Saddle River, NJ: Pearson Merrill Prentice Hall.

Nicholson, P. (2007). A history of e-learning. In B. Fernandez-Manjon, J. M. Sanchez-Perez, J. A. Gomez-Pulido, M. A. Vega-Rodriguez, and J. Bravo-Rodriguez (Eds.), *Computers and education: E-Learning, from theory to practice* (pp. 1–11). Dordrecht, The Netherlands: Springer.

Papert, S. (1994). *The children's machine: Rethinking school in the age of the computer*. New York: Basic Books.

Schank, R. (2002). *Designing world-class e-learning: How IBM, GE, Harvard Business School, and Columbia University are succeeding at e-learning*. New York: McGraw Hill.

EIGHT

Online and Blended Learning

OBJECTIVES

At the conclusion of the chapter, the reader will be able to:

1. Describe the strengths and weaknesses of online learning environments (ISTE 1, 2, 3, 5, 6).
2. Describe various types of learning activities and resources that can be used to create effective online learning environments (ISTE 1, 2, 3, 5, 6).
3. Identify the set of technology tools needed to design and implement an online course (ISTE 1, 2, 3, 6).
4. Describe strategies to promote student engagement with content in an online course (ISTE 2, 3, 5, 6).
5. Describe various approaches that can be used to promote productive peer interactions in an online setting (ISTE 2, 3, 5, 6).
6. Explain strategies instructors can use to promote learning and support community interactions (ISTE 2, 3, 5, 6).

OVERVIEW OF ONLINE AND BLENDED LEARNING

There was a time when students who could not enroll in a course in a traditional face-to-face setting had one other option for taking a course and receiving credit. They could sign up for a correspondence course. This was early "distance education." Schools mailed instructional materials and assignments to students, and students mailed completed assignments back to the school for grading. The process would repeat until students completed the correspondence course.

Today, distance education has grown significantly through the use of networked computer technologies. There are many fully online courses available now from universities for college-age and adult learners, including online versions of traditional classes as well as massive open online courses for the general public. Online courses are also offered as an alternative to traditional high school and middle school courses in many states. For the 2013–2014 school year, thirty states had fully online schools operating across the entire state. Approximately 315,000 students attended these fully online schools (Watson, Pape, Murin, Gemin, & Vashaw, 2014).

Online courses have become so successful that they are not viewed anymore as just a "distance education" option. Some students choose that format even when distance is not an issue. For example, residential college students on many campuses can choose a mix of traditional and online courses during the same semester. Online learning is considered by many experts to be one of the fastest growing trends in the educational use of technology (U.S. Department of Education, 2010). Helping ensure appropriate technologies are used to maximize learning is one of the roles of an educational leader as outlined by the Technical Standards and Safety Authority Technology Standards (see appendix C), and so school leaders should also aim to become more familiar with online learning.

While online courses can vary significantly in terms of quality, the best online course designs are superb, with multimedia instructional materials, interactive learning objects, asynchronous online discussions, synchronous video-conferencing sessions, and advanced assignment and assessment mechanisms in place. Most make use of learning management systems (LMS) like the ones discussed in chapter 7. Many employ supplementary online services for video, electronic books (ebooks), and other online content.

Comparing the best online course materials with paper-based correspondence course materials would be like comparing a trip in modern luxury car with leather seats, climate control, and GPS navigation to a trip in horse-drawn wagon with a set of paper maps. Both move people, but one does so much more comfortably and effectively. Examples of superb, publicly available online courses can be found in many places including edX.org and Coursera.org.

Benefits and Trade-offs of Online Learning

Online learning environments have many potential benefits. To begin, they provide students with greater flexibility and convenience. Regularly attending a face-to-face class can be difficult for some people. This can be related to regular travel from home to school or because of conflicts with other family or work responsibilities.

Students in an online environment can study and participate at any time of the day. Some online courses use synchronous meetings as well, and these can be facilitated through the use of video conferencing or virtual meeting software. Attending a virtual meeting from home requires a much smaller time and cost commitment than having to travel to attend a traditional class meeting.

Online courses often use video recordings, multimedia presentations, and asynchronous text-based online discussion forums. These elements are particularly good for students who would benefit from hearing explanations more than once. They can replay part of a lecture several times, for example, without worrying about annoying other students who just want the instructor to move on to the next topic.

Online discussion forums are often very good for "leveling the playing field" and encouraging quieter students to participate. Students do not need to be loud or feel the need to interrupt others to express their thoughts. A person's age, appearance, and social status are not relevant online. Everyone has an equal opportunity to share his or her points. Also, removing the pressure to respond immediately can sometimes elevate the quality of discussions, as it allows participants to think through their responses before sharing them.

There are also many well-known drawbacks. They are mostly related to the limited nature of online interactions compared to face-to-face situations. To begin, an online interaction lacks the rich verbal and nonverbal communication that can occur in a face-to-face setting. Body language and subtle facial expressions can convey a lot of nonverbal information.

Video conferencing and other technologies try to reduce this problem, but there is no technological equivalent to the vibrant and complex interpersonal interactions that can occur in a traditional face-to-face setting. Also, there are some learning activities, like a frog dissection for example, where the physical experience—the sights, sounds, smells, and tactile sensations—is important. Computer simulations may be able to replicate some of the sights and sounds, but the other sensations just cannot be captured with our current technology tools.

Also, online learning requires students to be more self-motivated and to be responsible for monitoring their own work and progress. Students who do not practice a certain minimal level of independence will not succeed in an online environment. In addition, online teaching appears to require skills that experienced face-to-face instructors do not necessarily possess. New online instructors need to develop and master online teaching skills.

Blended Learning

Blended learning (or hybrid learning) designs, are a mix of traditional classroom meetings with online course components. These designs attempt to include the benefits of traditional face-to-face classes, with some of the benefits of online classes. Flipped classroom lessons are an example of how teachers can incorporate a blended learning approach to their regular classes.

In a flipped math lesson for example, explanations of concepts that are traditionally delivered through a lecture or presentation are recorded and made available online. Students are asked to view the recordings at home. Class time is used for problem solving and discussion to help students apply the concepts with feedback and support from the teacher.

This is "flipped" in the sense that usually class time is used for the explanation of concepts, and students are asked to apply the concepts by solving practice problems for homework. The presence of a live teacher is more important during problem solving than for a concept explanation. Also, a recorded explanation can be viewed repeatedly by students who would benefit from hearing an explanation multiple times.

The primary mode of interaction in a flipped classroom implementation is still the face-to-face classroom time, and online components are meant to support better use of classroom time. A blended approach can be applied to courses in other ways as well. In some settings, the online component becomes the primary mode of interaction, with occasional face-to-face meetings used to support or supplement online interactions.

While there is no one required ratio of face-to-face to online meetings for something to be "blended," some organizations like the Sloan Consortium (2008) suggest that 30% to 80% of course content should be delivered online to be considered blended. Depending on the learning objectives and the audience, it is completely reasonable for different ratios to be chosen. Some studies have found that blended courses can lead to better learning outcomes than traditional face-to-face courses (U.S. Department of Education, 2010). This may be due to having the right mix of experiences in online and traditional situations to maximize the benefits of each setting.

DESIGNING ONLINE AND BLENDED LEARNING UNITS

Designing effective fully online courses, or online components to support blended courses, can be very challenging. While some studies suggest that online learning effectiveness can be comparable to learning in traditional face-to-face settings (U.S. Department of Education, 2010), the face-to-face approach is still seen as the gold standard. However, good online designs can provide many of the features of traditional courses in alternate ways, and even provide benefits available only through the online format.

Technology Platform and Tools

To begin designing online units, a dependable technology platform must first be chosen. Most popular LMSs like Blackboard and Moodle provide this platform. Many LMS services also offer course templates that provide a starting skeleton for designing online units.

For smaller online lessons or for developing online resources, less comprehensive platforms can also work. If sharing instructional handouts and homework files is all that is needed, Google Drive or some other file sharing service may be sufficient. If the sharing of recorded explanations for a flipped lesson implementation is all that is needed, services like Educreations or Screencast.com may be sufficient.

Tools for creating content for instructional units is also needed. Software and hardware combinations discussed in previous chapters can be used to create necessary text, graphics, video, or multimedia elements. Most LMSs will have the appropriate features needed to then include those elements into an online lesson or a fully online course.

The set of features provided by different LMSs can vary, but ideally, an online learning platform should be able to provide support for most of the following elements commonly found in online courses:

- Formatted text and graphics
- Mechanisms for providing access to ebooks and other online reading resources
- Embedded audio and video materials
- Asynchronous online discussions
- Synchronous online meetings with video conferencing, text chat, document sharing, meeting recording, and other features
- Synchronous online chat
- Assignment submission and grading
- Testing mechanisms
- Survey mechanisms
- Email or messaging

The ability to easily add formatted text and graphics to an online course is essential; they are the building blocks of any online course. An LMS should ideally permit a designer to embed access to electronic reading materials such as ebooks and PDF files, or at the very least enable the designer to provide hyperlinks to such resources. The ability to embed audio and video elements into course materials is also important. Creating a clean user experience is easier with this ability. Support of asynchronous online discussions is a staple of online courses and should continue to be well supported.

Synchronous online meetings complement the asynchronous discussions. Ideally, online meeting tools should be able to provide live video conferencing (or at least audio), screen sharing, file sharing, text chat, and meeting recording capabilities. Recorded meetings serve as a valuable resource for students who are unable to attend synchronously, and also for students wishing to review some of the material discussed during the meeting. Meeting platforms that require the use of separate telephone lines for audio are not as useful because they are unable to record full meetings.

The LMS itself does not need to have online meeting capabilities built into it. Outside services like Adobe Connect, Cisco WebEx, and Saba can be used to provide this capability. Hyperlinks to the online meeting can be embedded in the LMS course materials. Other online tools that provide live video options like Google Hangouts and Skype are useful too, but they have limitations (recording difficulties, number of participant restrictions) that make them less capable for full online meetings. Synchronous online text chat can serve as a useful supplement when full online meetings cannot be supported for bandwidth or other technical reasons.

Support for managing assignment submission and grading is essential. For example, the ability to use rubrics for grading is helpful for both instructors and students. Testing and survey mechanisms round out the list of features online learning platforms should provide. Full email services do not need to be provided by the LMS itself (although some do provide this), but providing some connection to school email systems through clickable hyperlinks can be helpful.

Pedagogical Theories and Models

Online learning is recognized as a subset of learning in general. So existing theories used in other settings apply to online learning as well (e.g., Ally, 2008). While the delivery mechanisms and modes of interaction have changed, the learners have not. Existing theories, strategies, and models can then be adapted to take into account the features and constraints of an online environment. Many successful online learning strategies are adaptations of successful face-to-face strategies.

Designers of new online learning units can start with pedagogical theories and strategies that are appropriate for their selected learning objectives. For example, a designer may decide that the most appropriate approach is a problem-based unit, a direct instruction–influenced unit, an inquiry-based unit, a cooperative learning unit, or something else. Then the designer must adapt the unit to fit the constraints of the online environment. Anderson (2008), for example, is one of many authors who examine existing theories and models and consider their implications for online learning.

A comprehensive review of all major theories and their implications for an online setting is beyond the scope of this chapter. However, one conceptual model of online learning is particularly useful. It is a frequently cited model called the "community of learning" model developed by Garrison, Anderson, and Archer (2000).

It is different in a sense from the pedagogical approaches just mentioned like problem-based learning or direct instruction. Rather than requiring the use of any particular sequence of teaching and learning events (like objectives, anticipatory set, guided practice, closure, etc.), this model points to essential characteristics that should be present in any online learning environment, regardless of the specific pedagogical approach used.

It is assumed in this model that the learning involves groups of people who are learning together. There are three component "presences" in the community of learning model (see figure 8.1):

- Cognitive presence
- Social presence
- Teaching presence

Cognitive presence is defined as the extent to which participants in a course are able to construct meaning (that is, learn) through sustained communication. Cognitive presence is considered the most basic element for success in a course setting and can be challenging for both face-to-face and online settings.

Social presence is the extent to which participants can project their personal characteristics into the course and be seen as "real people." This presence is primarily in support of cognitive presence. It is very important because learning often occurs more productively when participants find interacting with others in the group to be enjoyable and personally fulfilling. Participants are more likely to spend time on community learning activities when the social presence in a course is high.

Teaching presence is the extent to which (1) good instructional design ("structure") is present and (2) good instructional facilitation ("process") is present. Good instructional design includes the selection, organization, and presentation of content, assignments, and assessments for the course. In an online course, that includes the design of the online environment and materials. Design is usually the primary responsibility of the teacher. Good facilitation is the management of interactions during the course to promote better cognitive and social engagement. Facilitation is something that can be a shared responsibility between teachers and students.

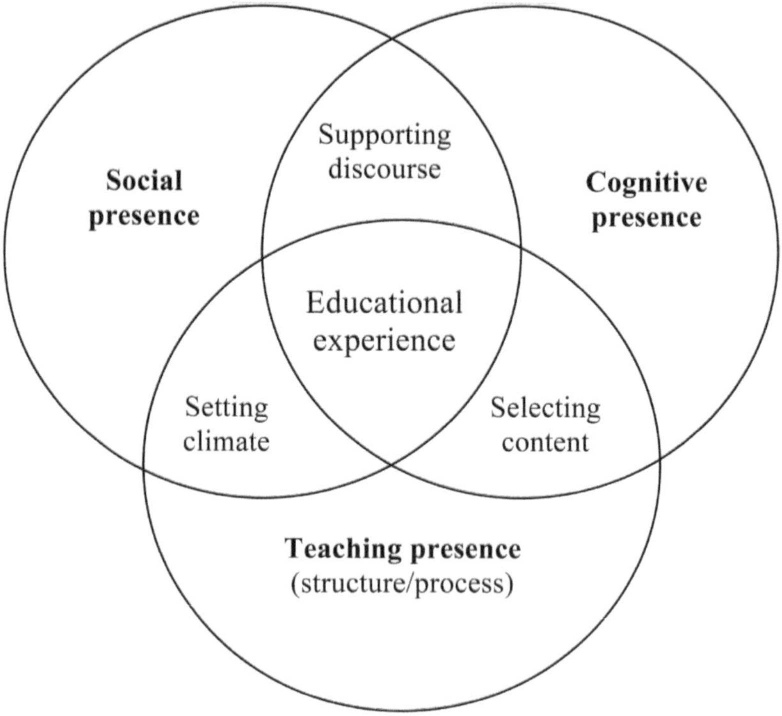

Figure 8.1. Three presences of the community of learning model.

The three components together determine the "educational experience" for students and, for a course to be effective, all three need to be present at sufficient levels. The three presences actually apply to all learning situations: traditional, online, and blended. However, teaching in a traditional setting sometimes doesn't require as much explicit attention to the three presences because some occur easily. On the other hand, because of the limitations imposed by the online environment, teaching online does require explicit attention to the three presences.

Various actions and design elements can have an effect on more than one presence at a time. As shown in figure 8.1, *selecting strong content* can have a positive effect on both cognitive presence and teaching presence. Adding components like discussion rules for critiquing others in a professional and friendly way helps set the climate and is a way to support discourse. This is a teaching action addressing "process" that can improve social presence and cognitive presence as well.

Designers of new online and blended learning units should consider and address the three presences regardless of the particular pedagogical approach being used. Effort should be made to maintain high enough levels of each presence through a careful design of the unit and through the teaching practices used by the online instructor. The next section discusses best practices and considers their influence on the three presences.

ONLINE AND BLENDED LEARNING BEST PRACTICES

Three types of interactions involve students in an online setting: student–content, student–student, and student–instructor (Anderson, 2008). Student–content interactions occur when students engage in reading, writing, reflecting, and otherwise working with the core content of a course. Student–student interactions are peer interactions that occur between students in a course through discussions, group projects, and other activities. Student–instructor interactions involve students talking to instructors, submitting assignments, receiving feedback, communicating in discussion boards, and so on.

Appropriately structuring, monitoring, and facilitating these interactions can lead to higher levels of the three presences and better overall student learning. Many existing theories and pedagogical models can be usefully applied to this design task for the online environment, leading to numerous implications. Experts often share these implications as sets of "best practices."

These best practices can be found in many forms in the literature related to the design of online learning environments (e.g., Boettcher, 2011; Shimoni, Barrington, Wilde, & Henwood, 2013; Siemens, 2002). The following sections of this chapter outline some of the more frequently mentioned best practices and discuss their significance.

Student–Content Interactions

Student–content interactions are at the core of an online course. It is when students thoughtfully and productively interact with the content that learning can occur. Reading texts, viewing videos, writing papers, and reflecting on ideas are all examples of student–content interactions. Some of the most frequently mentioned best practices for promoting more effective student–content interactions include the following:

1. Establish clear learning objectives.
2. Set clear expectations for online course participation.
3. Explain how the online environment works.

4. Design an online course structure that is clear and simple.
5. Provide navigation options that are simple and require as few clicks as possible to access important content.
6. Incorporate video for difficult concepts.
7. Provide a mix of resources and activities that incorporate a variety of large group, small group, and individual experiences.
8. Use simple assignments.
9. Make material as relevant as possible; develop questions and activities for students that relate to the students' experiences.
10. Encourage reflection.

Establishing clear learning objectives for students and establishing clear course participation expectations are closely related. Students need to know what they will learn from the course, and they need to know how they must participate to attain the appropriate level of learning. Clear expectations help students and instructors avoid problems in the future.

The next three practices are related to working with the online environment itself to enable interaction with the content. An explanation of how the online environment works should be provided, especially for new students. The level of required independent work and self-pacing needs to be communicated, as well as the nuts-and-bolts of finding readings and assignments. Explanations of this type can be minimized, if the structure of the online course is clear and simple to begin with. Navigation options should be intuitive and students should be able to get to core content areas with just a few mouse clicks.

The remaining best practices deal even more directly with content. Complex concepts should be explained using a variety of modalities, and videos provide a strong online medium for doing that. Videos can communicate ideas through a mix of text, images, animation, and audio, and they can be replayed as many times as necessary. Furthermore, a variety of other resources and activity types should be used to engage a potentially diverse group of students. Large group discussions, small group projects, and individual assignments should be a part of the mix.

However, the assignments themselves should actually be simple and easy to understand. The complexity of the content is what students should wrestle with, not the complexity of an assignment's instructions. Some assignment descriptions may become longer because of various assignment requirements. But the actual core description of what students need to do should be simple enough to be captured in just a few sentences.

An attempt should be made to make the material being learned as relevant and practical to students as possible. Activities and questions that are related to students' personal experiences will help students make mental connections that promote learning and interest. Mental connections will be further enhanced by encouraging students to regularly reflect on their learning and the relevance of what they are being asked to do.

Student–Student Interactions

Rich student–student interactions can make an online or blended course feel like a learning community. This is important because learning in community can increase participants' motivation, promote deeper learning, and lead to higher student satisfaction (Gannon-Leary & Fontainha, 2007). Many communication technology tools are currently available, including discussion boards, chat tools, and video conferencing tools. The skillful use of these tools can lead to stronger student–student interactions, which in turn enhances the social and cognitive presence of an online course.

Some frequently mentioned best practices and principles for promoting more effective student–student interactions include the following:

1. Provide motivating tasks.
2. Provide mechanisms for publicly sharing what is learned.
3. Create opportunities for reflective discussion of important concepts.
4. Prepare thought-provoking discussion questions; present conflicting opinions.
5. Provide sufficient time to engage in discussion and interaction.
6. Design interdependency of individuals for group work.
7. Establish the shared objective of advancing the collective knowledge.
8. Establish clear rules of personal conduct online.
9. Praise and model good discussant behavior.

A motivating task that is the central aim of a student community is essential in many learning community designs. Tasks can be motivating because they are connected to situations in the "real world" (e.g., Dewey, 1938) or because they deal with issues that students find personally relevant or interesting. For example, the assignment in an online science course may be to brainstorm solutions for some real problem like "reducing pollution in the local lake." Participants would engage in learning to better understand and address the problem.

The task could also be to further the state of knowledge for participants for some interesting topic like thunderstorms. This mirrors the activity of many scientific research communities where the pursuit of knowledge in some area (whether it has immediate practical application or not) is their motivating task. For online and blended courses, there may be one main motivating task that spans an entire semester or there may be a series of related motivating tasks that are addressed in sequence through assignments. Course materials should clearly identify and help promote the motivating task.

The public sharing of what is being learned can be very motivating for community members and lead to better learning as well. For example, instead of submitting assignments only to the instructor, students could be asked to share something interesting they created with the rest of the class through discussion board posts. A dedicated discussion board can be created for students to share interesting resources, videos, and documents they may have found or created.

The sharing of accomplishments can both help other community members learn, as well as enhance a participant's social status within the community. This is good because social goals have been found by many to be a big source of motivation (e.g., Urdan & Maehr, 1995). Additionally, sharing makes member conceptions public, enabling the community to comment and perhaps help refine this understanding.

Mechanisms for public sharing have an additional benefit: they often serve as a starting point for reflective discussion. One of the key benefits of learning within a community is the opportunity to give and receive helpful feedback. The thoughtful discussion of concepts within a supportive community can help refine ideas more effectively than an individual working alone.

Discussion can be further enhanced when thought-provoking questions, perhaps those presenting conflicting opinions, are provided. When these questions are addressed, the instructor should resist the urge to jump in too soon. Reflective horizontal student–student discussion is thought to have advantages over vertical student–teacher interactions (Hatano & Inagaki, 1991). In horizontal interactions, members are more likely to express a variety of ideas to examine and sort out together, because neither member is thought to possess the authoritative "right answer."

For rich, valuable student–student interactions to develop, sufficient time must be provided. Spending sufficient time on discussion and interaction leads to better student learning and achievement, and is necessary for developing the affective sense of belonging often attributed to a strong learning community. If there is a rush to jump too quickly from one topic to another, interactions can be superficial and less beneficial.

Designing interdependence into an assignment can be very valuable. Without some degree of interdependence, individuals could choose to complete every task alone. This precludes the benefits of being in a community. By designing interdependency into a task, members are encouraged to work together and participate as a group.

A number of lesson designs use interdependency. For example, cooperative learning designs like the "jigsaw" approach use interdependency.

Interdependent task structures not only encourage participants to work together externally, they can produce high levels of achievement and a stronger social presence for the course.

In strong learning communities, advancing everyone's collective knowledge is often a shared objective. People want other members of their community to be successful, too. In an online setting, this is a community norm that an instructor can try to establish through values communicated verbally and through the structure of activities.

In some activity design approaches, students are explicitly required to be both learners and peer teachers. Their objective may be to learn and to help their group members learn, so they can collectively perform a consequential task more skillfully. Examples of this include group projects where the skillful contribution of individuals benefits the entire group.

With interactions in any social setting (whether online or face to face), clear rules of personal conduct are important. The anonymity of the online setting can enable shy students to participate more effectively, but it can also lead to individuals expressing themselves in ways that are not appropriate. Explicit rules, modeling by the instructor, and regular feedback (including praise for good behavior) can help establish a positive environment for student–student interactions.

Student–Instructor Interactions

Student–instructor interactions are the interactions that occur between students and instructors at any time during the course. These include formal "teaching events" like a synchronous online meeting, to informal email messages from an instructor checking on the well being of a student. Healthy student–instructor interactions are essential for student learning and can set the tone for all other interactions. Some of the most frequently mentioned best practices for promoting more effective student–instructor interactions include the following:

1. Maintain an active online social presence; monitor the course.
2. Provide students with quick feedback.
3. Provide specific encouragement and meaningful feedback on assignments.
4. Provide opportunities for students to provide the instructor with early and regular formative feedback.
5. Provide a weekly "wrap-up" before next lesson begins.
6. Introduce a new week with an overview (including deadlines) of what is coming up.
7. Use the LMS (security and confidentiality issues).

Instructors are almost universally advised to maintain an active social presence in an online course. The course will not teach itself; it must be monitored and students need to know that the instructor is present. Recommendations for doing this include attempting to connect personally and emotionally with students early in the course, and checking in regularly each week with both content-related and personal comments.

Providing students with quick and meaningful feedback on assignments is another way to maintain an active presence in the course. Feedback that provides suggestions for improvement is more useful when it is received in time for students to make adjustments. It is also more useful when the assignment is still fresh on a student's mind.

Meaningful feedback should include specific encouragement from the instructor that highlights things the student did well. Feedback should not only be of the form that corrects errors, but should also be of the form that affirms and praises. Students who feel the instructor recognizes their strengths are more likely to accept suggestions for improvement and react positively to criticism.

In addition to the instructor providing feedback to students, students should be given the opportunity to provide formative feedback to the instructor. Early opportunities to receive feedback will give instructors enough time to make any necessary adjustments to the course. Some online experts even advise creating a safe place for students to complain. Complaints may initially be difficult to hear. But when valid complaints are addressed, this can lead to a more positive experience for everyone.

As part of an instructor's teaching role, providing a weekly "wrap-up" is often recommended as a practice that will help students organize what they are learning. Sometimes, discussions may wander in a direction where the conclusions are not clear to the student. A wrap-up by the instructor is another important form of instructional feedback that students can find valuable.

Providing an overview for the upcoming unit is a similar supervisory task. This can of course be embedded in the online course materials. But when an instructor provides this in a more personal way, it adds to the social presence and teaching presence of a course.

Finally, assuming a comprehensive LMS is used for the online course, there are many who advise using tools within the LMS for formal interactions that include discussions, assignments, grading, and other student–instructor communications. While there may be third-party tools that provide features that are preferred over the LMS version of a tool, when possible, staying within the course LMS is advised for reasons related to security and confidentiality.

When services are not available within an LMS, using other service providers may be necessary and advisable. For example, dedicated online meeting tools from third parties are often essential for online synchronous meetings. Security issues related to these services can often be addressed with the help of an organization's information technology staff.

LOOKING INTO THE FUTURE OF ONLINE LEARNING

Early films from the 1890s were often short recordings of circus acts, dancers, or sparring boxers. There was a fixed camera and people performed in front of the camera as they would before a live audience. People would then pay to view a short 30- to 60-second film (Dirks, n.d.). Motion pictures have developed significantly since then. Rather than creating recorded versions of what would normally be live entertainment, today's motion pictures offer an experience that simply cannot be replicated in any live setting.

Similarly, many early online learning designs attempted to provide online versions of live, face-to-face activities. These online substitutes were often not as good as the original face-to-face versions. However, online learning is moving in a direction similar to motion pictures, where online activities may provide a powerful experience that simply could not be replicated in a live setting. Continued work in this direction may result in engaging blended designs that incorporate the best experiences enabled by a live face-to-face setting, with the best experiences enabled by online settings.

There are already studies that show slight advantages of blended over completely face-to-face learning environments. As technology tools continue to improve, and the computing infrastructure in our schools continue to improve, future online and blended learning environments may cease to be inferior imitations of face-to-face learning. Instead, we may look forward to exciting online and blended learning environments that provide powerful interactive multimedia experiences mixed with rich community interactions that would have no purely live face-to-face equivalent.

SUMMARY

Online learning has become more than just a "distance education" option. With modern computer technology tools and refined teaching practices, the quality of online courses has improved significantly. Many higher education and K–12 organizations now use online learning environments for formal credit-bearing courses. There are also many free online course options for anyone interested in learning through organizations like edX

.org and Coursera.org. Online learning is seen as one of the fastest growing trends in the educational use of technology.

There are many potential benefits and well-known drawbacks to online learning environments. On the positive side, online courses provide students with greater flexibility and convenience. On the negative side, online interactions lack the rich verbal and nonverbal communication that can occur in a face-to-face setting.

Blended learning designs incorporate a mix of face-to-face and online components. These designs attempt to include the benefits of traditional face-to-face classes with some of the benefits of online classes. Some studies have found that blended courses can lead to better learning outcomes than traditional face-to-face courses.

Designing online and blended learning units can be very challenging. To begin, a dependable technology platform should be used to manage the online learning environment. Many popular LMSs like Blackboard and Moodle can provide this platform. Additional tools and online services can be used to create materials for an online course.

Many of the learning theories, models, and strategies used for face-to-face instruction can also be applied to the online environment, with the constraints of online kept in mind. Many successful online learning strategies are in fact adaptations of successful face-to-face strategies. When designing an online unit, an appropriate pedagogical strategy should be chosen first based on the learning objectives, and then appropriate online activities and tools can be used to implement the strategy.

A conceptual model that is particularly useful for thinking about the online learning environment is the "community of learning" model developed by Garrison, Anderson, and Archer (2000). In this model, three component "presences" are identified: cognitive presence, social presence, and teaching presence. The three components together determine the educational experience for students, and for a course to be effective, all three need to be present at sufficient levels.

Many existing theories and pedagogical models can be usefully applied to the online environment for design implications. Experts often share these implications in the form of "best practices." Some of the best practices shared in the literature for online learning include establishing clear learning objectives; providing a mix of large group, small group, and individual activities; encouraging reflection; providing mechanisms for sharing what is learned; and providing quick feedback.

Online learning is still in its early stages of development. As more interactive technologies become available and technology tool use becomes easier, the quality of online learning environments should improve even further. Future online and blended learning environments may tap into opportunities that face-to-face environments alone could not have possibly offered.

CASE STUDY

You are a high school teacher who has been asked to advise your school district on some possible future initiatives. One of those is the potential development of online or hybrid course options for mathematics.

The district would like to provide online or hybrid course options for some of the advanced math courses. The reasoning is that there may be too few students in one building to justify the creation of a class, but there may be enough students when many school building populations are considered together. The district would like to hear your thoughts. What kind of format would you recommend (online, hybrid, or none)? Why? What skills should a potential teacher for these courses have and what kind of training should be provided? Why?

The department is also considering the creation of online or hybrid introductory algebra course for students. The reasoning here is that many students struggle with algebra in a traditional face-to-face course, so perhaps an online setting may be helpful for these students. What kind of format would you recommend for an introductory algebra course (online, hybrid, or none)? Why? Should a completely separate and newly designed online hybrid algebra course be created, or would it better to try to incorporate online elements into existing face-to-face classes? Why?

EXERCISES AND DISCUSSION QUESTIONS

1. What are some of the strengths and weaknesses of an online learning environment?
2. For what subject matter might online courses, using current technology, be more appropriate? For what subject matter might online courses be less appropriate?
3. Conversations online can be supported using asynchronous discussions or synchronous online meetings. In what kinds of situations would one be preferred over another? What are the strengths of each approach?
4. Which of the three presences (cognitive, social, and teaching), seem to be inherently lower in an online setting? How might that presence be increased?
5. Several best practices for improving student–student interactions are described. Which of those have the most potential effect? What are some other practices that may improve student–student interactions?

REFERENCES

Ally, M. (2008). Foundations of educational theory for online learning. In T. Anderson (Ed.), *The theory and practice of online learning* (pp. 15–44). Edmonton, AB: AU Press.

Anderson, T. (2008). Towards a theory of online learning. In T. Anderson (Ed.), *The theory and practice of online learning* (pp. 45–74). Edmonton, AB: AU Press.

Boettcher, J. (2011). *Ten best practices for teaching online: Quick guide for new online faculty.* Retrieved from http://www.designingforlearning.info/services/writing/ecoach/tenbest.html

Dewey, J. (1938). *Experience and education.* New York: Macmillan.

Dirks, T. (n.d.). The history of film: The pre-1920s. *Filmsite.* Retrieved from http://www.filmsite.org/pre20sintro.html

Gannon-Leary, P., and Fontainha, E. (2007). Communities of practice and virtual learning communities: Benefits, barriers and success factors. *Barriers and Success Factors: eLearning Papers,* (5).

Garrison, D. R., Anderson, T., and Archer, W. (2000). Critical thinking in text-based environment: Computer conferencing in higher education. *The Internet and Higher Education,* 2(2), 87–105.

Hatano, G., & Inagaki, K. (1991). Sharing cognition through collective comprehension activity. In Resnick, L., Levine, J., and Teasley, S. (Eds.), *Perspectives on socially shared cognition.* Washington, DC: American Psychological Association.

Shimoni, R., Barrington, G., Wilde, R., & Henwood, S. (2013). Addressing the needs of diverse distributed students. *International Review of Research in Open and Distance Learning, 14*(3), 134–157.

Siemens, G. (2002). *Lessons learned teaching online.* Retrieved from http://www.elearnspace.org/Articles/lessonslearnedteaching.htm

Sloan Consortium. (2008). *Staying the course: Online education in the United States.* Retrieved from http://www.onlinelearningsurvey.com/reports/staying-the-course.pdf

U.S. Department of Education. (2010). *Evaluation of evidence-based practices in online learning: A meta-analysis and review of online learning studies.* Retrieved from http://www2.ed.gov/rschstat/eval/tech/evidence-based-practices/finalreport.pdf

Urdan, T., & Maehr, M. (1995). Beyond a two-goal theory for motivation and achievement: A case for social goals. *Review of Educational Research, 65*(3) 213–243.

Watson, J., Pape, L., Murin, A., Gemin, B., & Vashaw, L. (2014). *Keeping pace with K–12 digital learning: An annual review of policy and practice.* Retrieved from http://www.kpk12.com/wp-content/uploads/EEG_KP2014-fnl-lr.pdf

Appendix A

School Technology Resource Websites

American Educational Research Association (AERA):
http://www.aera.net/
American Technology Education Association
http://ateaonline.org
Annenberg Institute
http://annenberginstitute.org/
ASCD (Association for Supervision and Curriculum Development)
http://www.ascd.org
Association for Educational Communications and Technology (AECT)
http://www.aect.org
Association of School Business Officials International (ASBOI)
http://www.asbointl.org
Carnegie Foundation for the Advancement of Teaching
http://www.carnegiefoundation.org/
Center for Safe Schools
http://www.safeschools.info/emergency-management
Center for Technology in Learning
http://www.sri.com/about/organization/education/ctl
Closing the Achievement Gaps
http://www.edtrust.org/dc/press-room/press-release/states-can-close-the-achievement-gap-by-decades-end-new-education-trust-
Consortium for School Networking (CoSN)
http://www.cosn.org/
Education Commission of the States
http://www.ecs.org
Education Leadership Improves Student Learning
http://www.wallacefoundation.org/knowledge-center/school-leadership/Pages/default.aspx
Education Week: Technology
http://www.edweek.org/topics/technology/

Great Schools by Design
http://www.archfoundation.org/category/featured-programs/great-schools-by-design/
International Society of the Learning Sciences (ISLS)
https://isls.org/
International Society for Technology in Education
http://www.iste.org
Keeping Pace with K–12 Digital Learning
http://www.kpk12.com/
MacArthur Foundation: Digital Media and Learning
http://www.macfound.org/programs/learning/
National Center for Educational Statistics (NCES)
http://nces.ed.gov
National Clearinghouse for Educational Facilities
http://www.ncef.org
National Conference of State Legislatures (NCSL)
http://www.ncsl.org
No Child Left Behind
http://www.ed.gov/nclb/
Online Learning Consortium (OLC), formerly the Sloan Consortium
http://onlinelearningconsortium.org/
Teacher and Leader Effectiveness
http://www.doe.k12.ga.us/School-Improvement/Teacher-and-Leader-Effectiveness/Pages/default.aspx
Teacher Leader Model Standards
http://teacherleaderstandards.org/
Teacher Leader Voice and Capacity Building Lead to Student Growth
http://www.edwardsedservices.com/teacher-leader-voice-and-capacity-building-lead-to-student-growth/
U.S. Department of Education
http://www.ed.gov
U.S. Department of Education Office of Educational Technology
http://tech.ed.gov/

Appendix B

Common Technology Acronyms

AC	alternating current
AM	amplitude modulation
ATX	Advanced Technology eXtended
BD	Blu-ray disk
CD	compact disk
CHAP	challenge handshake authentication protocol
CLI	command line interface
CPU	central processing unit
CRT	cathode ray tube
DC	direct current
DHCP	dynamic host configuration protocol
DIMM	dual in-line memory module
DLP	digital light processing
DOS	disk operating system
DoS	denial of service
DRAM	dynamic random access memory
DSL	digital subscriber line
DVD	digital video disk
DVI	digital video interface
EAP	extensible authentication protocol
EDVAC	electronic discrete variable automatic computer
EMF	electromotive force
ENIAC	electronic numeric integrator and computer
eSATA	external serial advanced technology attachment
exe	executable
FET	field effect transistor
FM	frequency modulation
FTP	file transfer protocol

GPU	graphic processing unit
HDD	hard disk drive
HDMI	high-definition multimedia interface
HP	Hewlett-Packard
IBM	International Business Machines
IC	integrated circuit
IDS	intrusion detection system
IOS	internetwork operating system
IP	Internet protocol
IPS	intrusion prevention system
ISP	Internet service providers
IT	information technology
L2TP	layer 2 tunneling protocol
LAN	local area networks
LCD	liquid crystal display
LED	light-emitting diode
LMS	learning management systems
mA	milliamperes
MAC	media access control
MAN	metropolitan area networks
MIDI	musical instructional digital interface
MOOC	massive open online course
MOSFET	metal-oxide semiconductor field-effect transistor
NIC	network interface card
OS	operating system
PAP	password authentication protocol
PC	personal computer
PIV	peak inverse voltage rating
PLA	programmable logic array
POP	post office protocol
PPTP	point-to-point tunneling protocol
PSU	power supply unit
RAM	random access memory
ROM	read-only memory
SIMM	single in-line memory module
SMTP	simple mail transfer protocol
SRAM	static random access memory
SSD	solid-state drive
SSID	service set identifier

SYN	synchronize
TCP/IP	transmission control protocol/Internet protocol
U	enriched uranium
UHD-TV	ultra-high-definition television
UPS	uninterrupted power supplies
USB	universal serial bus
VCSEL	vertical cavity surface emitting lasers
VGA	video graphics array
VoIP	voice over Internet protocol
VPN	virtual private network
VPU	visual processing unit
WAN	wide area networks
WAP	wireless access point
WNIC	wireless network interface card
WWW	World Wide Web
Ω	omega (Greek)

Appendix C

Technology Standards for School Administrators: TSSA Framework, Standards, and Performance Indicators (v4.0)

I. **Leadership and Vision**—Educational leaders inspire a shared vision for comprehensive integration of technology and foster an environment and culture conducive to the realization of that vision.

Educational leaders:

A. facilitate the shared development by all stakeholders of a vision for technology use and widely communicate that vision.
B. maintain an inclusive and cohesive process to develop, implement, and monitor a dynamic, long-range, and systemic technology plan to achieve the vision.
C. foster and nurture a culture of responsible risk-taking and advocate policies promoting continuous innovation with technology.
D. use data in making leadership decisions.
E. advocate for research-based effective practices in the use of technology.
F. advocate on the state and national levels for policies, programs, and funding opportunities that support implementation of the district technology plan.

II. **Learning and Teaching**—Educational leaders ensure that curricular design, instructional strategies, and learning environments integrate appropriate technologies to maximize learning and teaching.

Educational leaders:

A. identify, use, evaluate, and promote appropriate technologies to enhance and support instruction and standards-based curriculum leading to high levels of student achievement.
B. facilitate and support collaborative technology-enriched learning environments conducive to innovation for improved learning.
C. provide for learner-centered environments that use technology to meet the individual and diverse needs of learners.

D. facilitate the use of technologies to support and enhance instructional methods that develop higher-level thinking, decision-making, and problem-solving skills.
E. provide for and ensure that faculty and staff take advantage of quality professional learning opportunities for improved learning and teaching with technology.

III. Productivity and Professional Practice—Educational leaders apply technology to enhance their professional practice and to increase their own productivity and that of others.

Educational leaders:
A. model the routine, intentional, and effective use of technology.
B. employ technology for communication and collaboration among colleagues, staff, parents, students, and the larger community.
C. create and participate in learning communities that stimulate, nurture, and support faculty
D. and staff in using technology for improved productivity.
E. engage in sustained, job-related professional learning using technology resources.
F. maintain awareness of emerging technologies and their potential uses in education.
G. use technology to advance organizational improvement.

IV. Support, Management, and Operations—Educational leaders ensure the integration of technology to support productive systems for learning and administration.

Educational leaders:
A. develop, implement, and monitor policies and guidelines to ensure compatibility of technologies.
B. implement and use integrated technology-based management and operations systems.
C. allocate financial and human resources to ensure complete and sustained implementation of the technology plan.
D. integrate strategic plans, technology plans, and other improvement plans and policies to align efforts and leverage resources.
E. implement procedures to drive continuous improvement of technology systems and to support technology replacement cycles.

V. Assessment and Evaluation—Educational leaders use technology to plan and implement comprehensive systems of effective assessment and evaluation.

Educational leaders:

A. use multiple methods to assess and evaluate appropriate uses of technology resources for learning, communication, and productivity.
B. use technology to collect and analyze data, interpret results, and communicate findings to improve instructional practice and student learning.
C. assess staff knowledge, skills, and performance in using technology and use results to facilitate quality professional development and to inform personnel decisions.
D. use technology to assess, evaluate, and manage administrative and operational systems.

VI. Social, Legal, and Ethical Issues—Educational leaders understand the social, legal, and ethical issues related to technology and model responsible decision-making related to these issues.

Educational leaders:

A. ensure equity of access to technology resources that enable and empower all learners and educators.
B. identify, communicate, model, and enforce social, legal, and ethical practices to promote responsible use of technology.
C. promote and enforce privacy, security, and online safety related to the use of technology.
D. promote and enforce environmentally safe and healthy practices in the use of technology.
E. participate in the development of policies that clearly enforce copyright law and assign ownership of intellectual property developed with district resources.

Source: These standards are the property of the TSSA Collaborative and may not be altered without written permission. The following notice must accompany reproduction of these standards: "This material was originally produced as a project of the Technology Standards for School Administrators Collaborative." Foundation Standards Developed by the TSSA Collaborative Draft v4.0 4 Draft Date 11/5/01.

Appendix D

Trademarks

The following trademarks are listed in the book. They have been listed here in alphabetical order.

Adobe Photoshop, Photoshop Elements, Premiere, Portable Document Format (PDF), and Connect are registered trademarks of Adobe Systems Inc.
ALSoft is a registered trademark of ALSoft, Inc.
Android, Google, Google Drive, Google Docs, Presentation, YouTube, Hangouts, Chrome, Chromebook, Chromecast, Googlecast and Drive are trademarks of Google Inc.
Apache and OpenOffice are trademarks of The Apache Software Foundation.
Apple, iPhone, iPad, iPad Air, Mac, Macintosh, MacBook, MacBook Pro, FireWire, OSX, AppleTV, Apple II, MacOS X, Keynote, Pages, Numbers, iMovie, and Final Cut Pro are registered trademarks of Apple, Inc.
ASP.NET is a trademark of Microsoft Corporation.
Avanquest is a registered trademark of Avanquest North America, Inc.
Blackboard is a registered trademark of Blackboard, Inc.
Bluetooth is a trademark of Bluetooth SIG, Inc.
Blu-ray is a registered trademark of Sony Corp.
Blu-ray Disc (BD) is a registered trademark of the Blu-ray Disc Association (BDA).
Bubbl.us is a trademark of LKCollab, LLC.
Canon is a registered trademark of Canon Inc.
Carnegie Learning is a registered trademark of Carnegie Learning, Inc.
CD Compact Disk is a trademark of Phillips
Cisco WebEx is a registered trademark of Cisco Systems, Inc.
Cmap is a trademark of IHMC.
DLP is a registered trademark of Texas Instruments.
Dow Jones Industrial Average is a trademark of Dow Jones & Company, Inc.
Dropbox is a registered trademark of Dropbox Inc.
DVD is a trademark of DVD Format/Logo Licensing Corporation.
DVI is a registered trademark of Digital Display Working Group.
Educreations is a trademark of Educreations, Inc.
edX is a registered trademark of edX Inc.
Epson is a registered trademark of Seiko Epson Corporation.
eSATA is a trademark of Wiebe Tech LLC.

Ethernet is a registered trademark of Xerox Corp.
Fairchild is a registered trademark *of* Fairchild Semiconductor Corp.
Firefox is a registered trademark of the Mozilla Foundation.
Geometer's Sketchpad is a registered trademark of Key Curriculum Press.
GIMP is a trademark of The GIMP Development Team.
Haiku Deck is a trademark of Haiku Deck, Inc.
HDMI is a registered trademark of HDMI Licensing, LLC.
Hewlett-Packard and HP are registered trademarks of Hewlett-Packard Development Company, LP.
IBM and IBM PC are registered trademarks of International Business Machines, Inc.
IBM System/360 and IBM System/370 are trademarks of International Business Machines, Inc.
IEEE 1394 is a trademark of The Institute of Electrical and Electronics Engineers Standards Association.
Intel, Pentium, and Thunderbolt are registered trademarks of Intel Corp.
iOS is a registered trademark of Cisco and used under license by Apple Inc.
Java and JavaScript are trademarks of Oracle Corp.
LCoS is a trademark of Brillian Corp.
LibreOffice is a trademark of the Document Foundation.
Linux is a registered trademark of Linus Torvalds.
Litmos is a registered trademark of Callidus Software Inc.
MacOS X Yosemite is a trademark of Apple, Inc.
Malwarebytes and Malwarebytes Anti-Malware are registered trademarks of Malwarebytes Corp.
Mastery Manager and Goldstar Learning are trademarks of Goldstar Learning Inc.
Math Blaster is a registered trademark of Vivendi Universal Publishing.
Microsoft, Microsoft Office, PowerPoint, Word, Outlook, Excel, Microsoft Windows, Windows 7, Windows 8, and Windows 10 are registered trademarks of Microsoft Corp.
Moodle is a registered trademark of the Moodle Trust.
Movie Maker is a trademark of Microsoft Corporation.
National Geographic is a trademark of National Geographic Society.
NeoOffice is a registered trademark of Planamesa Inc.
Nessus is a registered trademark of Tenable Network Security, Inc.
Northwest Evaluation Association and MAP are registered trademarks of NWEA.
Paintshop Pro is a registered trademark of JASC Corp.
Pasco Scientific is a registered trademark of PASCO scientific.
Perl is a registered trademark of the Perl Foundation.
PhET is a trademark owned by the Regents of the University of Colorado.
Pixlr Editor is a registered trademark of Autodesk, Inc.
Prezi is a registered trademark of Prezi, Inc.
Prosoft Engineering is a registered trademark of Prosoft Engineering, Inc.
Python is a registered trademark of the PSF (Python Software Foundation).
SABA is a registered trademark of Thomsom Corp.
Sakai is a registered trademark of the Sakai Foundation.

Samsung and Samsung Galaxy Tab are registered trademarks of Samsung Electronics Co., Ltd.
Scantron and Performance Series are registered trademarks of Scantron Corp.
Schoology is a registered trademark of Schoology, Inc.
Sketchbook is a registered trademark of Autodesk, Inc.
Skype is a trademark of Skype Limited.
Sumo Paint is a trademark of the Sumoware, Ltd.
Super Anti-Spyware is a registered trademark of Support.com, Inc.
Symantec is a registered trademark of Symantec Corp.
Texas Instruments is a registered trademark of Texas Instruments Corp.
Toshiba is registered trademark of Toshiba Corporation.
University of Chicago is a registered trademark of University of Chicago.
Vernier is a registered trademark of Vernier Software & Technology LLC.
Video Graphics Array and VGA are trademarks of International Business Machines Corp.
WeVideo is a trademark of WeVideo, Inc.
Wi-Fi is a trademark of the Wi-Fi Alliance.
Word Perfect is a registered trademark of Corel Corp.

Index

About the Authors

Samuel M. Kwon is a Concordia University Chicago faculty member and teaches courses in the Educational Technology program. His primary areas of research include technology-supported teaching and learning, online learning, and the design of learning environments. He has a PhD from Northwestern University in Education and Social Policy—Learning Sciences, and an MS and BS from MIT in Electrical Engineering and Computer Science. He has published many articles on teaching, learning, and the use of technology.

Dan Tomal is Distinguished Professor of Leadership at Concordia University and has published eighteen books (most with Rowman & Littlefield Education) and over two hundred articles studies and articles. He is a former administrator, high school and university technology teacher, and corporate consultant. He has made guest appearances on many national and local television and radio shows such as *CBS This Morning, NBC Cover to Cover,* ABC, *Les Brown, Joan Rivers,* and *Chicago Talks,* among others.

Aram S. Agajanian, PhD, is a professor and has served as a chair of electronics and computer engineering technology programs in several institutions. His expertise is in the fields of electrical, computer, biomedical engineering technology, and network communications. He has published numerous articles on educational leadership; the papers concentrate on encouraging female enrollment in science, technology, engineering, and math programs. He is the co-author (with D. Tomal) of *Electronic Troubleshooting.*

www.ingramcontent.com/pod-product-compliance
Ingram Content Group UK Ltd.
Pitfield, Milton Keynes, MK11 3LW, UK
UKHW012040150926
475560UK00001B/104

9 781475 815